Seasonal Resistance

Rabbi Mike Moskowitz

To my son Nachi, whose joyful existence is a
constant act of resistance.

Contents

Tishri

Cheshvan

Kislev

Tevet

Shvat

Adar

Acknowledgments

We are told that when we arrive in the heavenly study hall, we will be asked, "Did you set fixed times for Torah study?[1]— קָבַעְתָּ עִתִּים לַתּוֹרָה".[2] Congregation Beit Simchat Torah has provided not only a platform to learn and teach Torah, but also the opportunity to be part of a community that has so much wisdom to offer the world. All of the Torah in this book has been energized and influenced by my experiences at CBST.

Avigayil Halpern, Cooperberg-Rittmaster Pastoral and Educational Intern, offered many editorial suggestions, enriching this book. I'm so grateful for your support and excited for how your rabbinate will impact the world! The cover design is by Sarah Berman & Josh Walker for Cluny Sorbonne Media. Your encouraging professionalism has made this process so enjoyable.

---

[1] Shabbat 31a.
[2] Additionally it can be understood as "Did you establish that each moment was attached to Torah".

In the Shema,[3] we accept upon ourselves to teach children[4] Torah, and also to study Torah all the time—at home and on the road, at night and in the morning. The verse juxtaposes teaching and learning because the best way to teach Torah to others is by taking the time ourselves to study it,[5] and then to speak about what we are learning.[6] Words can not describe the deep gratitude, and ever expanding appreciation I have for Rabbi Sharon Kleinbaum, the Clergy team, Board, Tasha, and all of the administrative support that makes being here possible, and also incredibly rewarding.

I have been blessed my whole life to journey with amazing people and witness how they have encountered and overcome adversity. Everyday I'm inspired by those who have refused to give up on the struggle.

My dear friends at Bayit: Rachel, David, Steve, Dara, Pamela and Cyn have been steady and creative thought partners, as well as holy enablers of my writing finding a home on the Bayit platform. Their pure passion, and reliable enthusiasm, builds welcoming structures of goodness that benefit everyone.

I'm eternally grateful to everyone who has supported, encouraged, and believed in me along the way. It has made all of the difference. Over the last four years, I have been privileged to be part of a spectacular cohort of rabbis at the Shalom Hartman Institute. An enormous investment of care and thoughtfulness has created a network of close friendships that have deeply enriched my life, well

---

[3] Deuteronomy 6:7.
[4] Rashi explains that "children" in this verse is referring to students.
[5] The best way to fulfill "וְשִׁנַּנְתָּם לְבָנֶיךָ" is through "וְדִבַּרְתָּ בָּם".
[6] See Rav Nosson Gestetner on Chinuch.

beyond the rabbinate. A very special thank you to Rabbi Lauren Berkun who models sensitive intentionality and grace.

My holy partner in life and living, R' Wendy, is the source of so much kindness and encouraging goodness in the universe. Each day together is a nourishing blessing of light that drives me to be a better human.

The Torah provides the healing answers to the urgent questions of the next generation—"אַרְבָּעָה בָנִים דִּבְּרָה תוֹרָה כְּנֶגֶד"[7]—My children continue to inspire and motivate me to learn more—for and from them. Their questions and lived experiences have also inspired and animated the Torah contained in this book. I only wish that my contributions of thought are as deserving as their holy offerings of being.

וְעַל הַכֹּל 'ה אֱלֹקֵינוּ אֲנַחְנוּ מוֹדִים לָךְ וּמְבָרְכִים אוֹתָךְ.

For all, Hashem, our God, we thank you and bless you.[8]

Of all the good to acknowledge and be thankful for, we single out that "Hashem is our God" and focus our gratitude on being able to be in relationship with Hashem. Even in the most difficult and darkest of times, knowing that we are not alone is a tremendous comfort and source of hope. May we all be sustained[9] with the optimism of opportunities, conscious that the time[10] for change is always now.

---

[7] From the Passover Haggadah—"the Torah speaks in response to the four children."

[8] From the grace after meals.

[9] מזן
[10] זמן

Foreword by Rabbi Sharon Kleinbaum

Working with Rabbi Mike Moskowitz as a colleague, beloved friend and teacher in my life and at Congregation Beit Simchat Torah, calls forth from me a number of Jewish blessings.

I recite the blessing for the presence of a great scholar, "for God has given a piece of God's own wisdom to those who stand in awe of God." Mike's every breath reflects continuous Jewish learning and the awe of God. This is a blessing to all who are in Mike's presence and are lucky enough to learn from him. His teachings take my breath away and simultaneously give me a reassurance that allows me to breathe easier.

Mike's teaching in this book, as in all of his teaching, does more than sound a call for social justice from the deep truths of traditional Jewish texts. He demonstrates how the magical, cross-millennial conversation of the rabbis/meforshim/commentators make a vision of progressive values inevitable. I know no one in the Jewish world who can speak so organically with both scholarly and moral authority about the justice of racial, gender, and LGBTQ equality. For this I would recite the blessing for seeing extraordinary beauty in the world. I bless God, that there is such as Mike in God's world.

We live in an era of emergencies. The planet itself, the principles of democracy that shield us from tyrants, the freedom to walk the world without fear of vigilante violence, the social contract rooted in a belief that every person is created in God's image—these are all under attack. Yet even in these terrifying times, I say a *shehecheyanu* that I have lived to see a rabbi who knows what Mike knows, speaks out and loud about what Mike believes, and in a voice that commands attention and respect in all corners of the Jewish world.

Introduction

The Oral Torah[11] begins with a question about time: "מֵאֵימָתַי—when". This question frames the entirety of the Mishnah until the last word: "בְּשָׁלוֹם—with peace". The first letter of each of the six orders of the Mishnah: זרעים, מועד, נשים, נזיקין, קדשים, טהרות form the phrase "זמן נקט". Perhaps Rebbe, the compiler of the Mishnah,[12] is responding to the implied question of "מֵאֵימָתַי בְּשָׁלוֹם—when will we be at peace?" answering "זמן נקט—it takes time." Not that we need to wait for it, but that time itself is the tool to achieve it. Learning Torah assists in teaching us how to best use each moment to heal and perfect this world.

Time is a creation; as it says "בְּרֵאשִׁית בָּרָא—a beginning was created".[13] There is a texture to time that, with developed

---

[11] Mishnah Berachot 1:1.
[12] Rebbe Yehudah HaNassi, the redactor of the Mishnah.
[13] Genesis 1:1.

sensitivity, can be felt and appreciated. It is also intended to inform and guide our efforts throughout our lives, as the verse in Ecclesiastes teaches, "לְכֹל־חֵפֶץ תַּחַת הַשָּׁמָיִם לַכֹּל זְמָן וְעֵת"—Everything has its season, and there is a time for everything under the heaven".[14]

Our lives are described by King David as but a handbreadth long.[15] It doesn't matter how long any of us live, we can only experience the moment at hand. Perhaps this is why, in Kohelet, there are fourteen—the numerical value for hand, יד—"times" mentioned for good, and another fourteen "times" that are not good.[16]

Judaism teaches that we have the power to harness every moment for holiness. This is reflected in the word for power—כח, having the numerical value of 28.[17] The best way to reclaim the time, as a lover of days,[18] is by doing good in the place of bad. All day, every day.

These seven verses in Kohelet[19] correspond to the seven days of the week, with each verse naming four distinct "times". This comes to include the day and the night, each having their own potential to be used for good, or the opposite.[20] It also acknowledges that there are cycles of time within other cycles of time, like the twenty-eight years that it takes for the sun to return to its original position.

---

[14] Ecclesiastes 3:1.
[15] Psalms 39:6.
[16] In Ecclesiastes 3:2–8 the word "עֵת" appears 28 times.
[17] See Chaim V'Shalom page 120.
[18] Psalms 34:13.
[19] Ecclesiastes 3:2–8.
[20] See Rokeach.

A time for peace, "עֵת שָׁלוֹם", is the last of the twenty-eight times mentioned because that is the ultimate goal; to achieve peace. It is how we conclude every prayer, kaddish, and priestly blessing.

When Jacob comes to bless Joseph's two sons, Menashe and Ephraim, he privileges Ephraim, the younger son, by placing his right hand on Ephraim's head while putting his left hand on Menashe's.[21] Joseph attempts to correct his father by taking his hand and repositioning it,[22] but is overruled.[23]

This disagreement can be understood as a dispute over which attribute, represented by each child, should be prioritized. Joseph names his first son Menashe because "God has made me forget my hardship"[24] and emphasizes a removal of the negativity.[25] By contrast, Ephraim receives his name from a recognition that "God has made me fertile in the land of my affliction",[26] highlighting the positive.

King David situates first moving away from the bad and then leaning into the good, before requesting peace and pursuing it,[27] "סוּר מֵרָע וַעֲשֵׂה־טוֹב בַּקֵּשׁ שָׁלוֹם וְרָדְפֵהוּ". By choosing Ephraim, Jacob is acting in the reverse order, choosing good and then moving away from bad.[28] King David and our ancestor Jacob represent two different approaches in how one uses time in spiritual practice.

---

[21] Genesis 48:14.
[22] Genesis 48:17.
[23] Genesis 48:19.
[24] Genesis 41:51.
[25] See Meyer Enie Chachamim on Yom Kippur.
[26] Genesis 41:52.
[27] Psalms 34:15.
[28] See Mei Sheloach.

Ephraim has his source in the earthy lowliness of "I am but dust and ashes".[29] Menashe, in Hebrew מנשה, is an anagram for "soul—נשמה"—and aligns with supernal pursuits. Is it better to focus on elevating Earth to Heaven, or bringing Heaven to Earth?

Procedurally, it seems, we are generally instructed to first disconnect from the negativity to free ourselves and be available to attach in positive ways. There are, however, particular times that the opposite approach is more appropriate. Elevating the physical to a level of spirituality is the path that Jacob argues best supports our holy struggle of perfecting this world.

Not coincidentally, the night of Passover[30] (also known as the night of order—*leil seder*) begins with *Kadesh* (sanctify) and is then followed by *Urchatz* (washing away the impurities). In times of clarity, opposing the bad is best achieved by replacing it with the good. Restoring justice is the ultimate form of resistance against the unjust.

"לַעֲשׂוֹת לַ'ה הֵפֵרוּ תּוֹרָתֶךָ עֵת"—It is a time to act for the LORD, for they have violated Your teaching".[31] Time, when not engaged with intentionally, is a rejection of tradition. It is described in rabbinic literature[32] "as the broken vessel that requires artisanal care to fix".

This is the work that we are expected to toil in, and is alluded to in the word "עת" standing for "עבודה תורה".[33]

---

[29] Genesis 18:27 "עָפָר וָאֵפֶר"—Ephraim is the plural of *efer*.
[30] The night when Jacob received his blessings from Isaac.
[31] Psalms 119:126.
[32] See the writing of R' Moshe Dovid Veli.
[33] Literally "Torah is the work" quoted in *seforim*.

Judaism is a religion of action and the question is always "now what?". The Hebrew word for "now—עתה" is grounded in time—the root "*et*" means time—and it is certainly a gift. The first time that "עתה" appears in the Hebrew Bible is when we are being expelled from the garden.[34] The *midrash* frames the "עתה" as "now we are invited to come back": אֵין וְעַתָּה אֶלָּא תְּשׁוּבָה—the words "and now" always mean a return.[35] Adam and Eve were formed in the utopian paradise of the Garden of Eden. We were born into a world already broken. We are here to use our time to navigate a return to the garden, this time as a co-creator.

---

[34] Genesis 3:22.
[35] Berishet Rabbah 21:6.

Nisan

Passover: Achieving the Ideal[36]

If Purim is the holiday of making do, then Passover, by contrast, is about achieving the ideal. The Jews are in a sorry state at the start of the Purim story—dispersed among the nations and isolated from one another. While we celebrate the foiling of Haman's evil plan by the end of the megillah, the Jewish people are still scattered in exile and potentially vulnerable to the next tyrant once Esther and Mordechai's influence wanes. On Purim, the people celebrate by sending gifts of food to one another because they cannot actually be together. While Esther has used her sway with the King to great effect, at the end of the book she is still married to a foreign king

---

[36] Originally published on March 26, 2021 for HBI and co-authored with Rabba Wendy Amsellem.

whom she did not choose, and the rule that every man dominates his wife is still very much the law of the land.

On Passover, the Israelites don't just demand better conditions for their servitude. Instead, they emerge as free people, heads held high, bedecked with the finery of their oppressors, as they sing their way to liberation. On Passover, there are no compromises. Moses demands that not a single Israelite, neither young nor old, neither female nor male, be left behind.[37]

When the rabbis describe the Exodus, they highlight gender equality as a striking feature. Both women and men receive reparations from the Egyptians. Both women and men rejoice at the splitting of the sea. It is specifically in the merit of the righteous women that all of Israel is redeemed.[38] This gender parity is further highlighted in the laws of the Seder night. Even though *halachah*[39] generally releases women from time-bound obligations, women are commanded to fully participate in the Seder. Women and men are both obligated to eat matzah, to drink four cups of wine, and to retell the story of the Exodus.

Shifting from a posture of coping to one of change requires leaning (pun intended) into different aspects of being human. The name for the first human, Adam—אדם, famously has its roots in "from the earth"[40] אֲדָמָה—literally grounded in the reality of the present and limited to whatever is available at the moment. However, Adam/אדם also has its source in the word אֲדַמֶּה, which means to

---

[37] Exodus 10:9.
[38] Talmud Bavli Sotah 11b.
[39] Jewish Law.
[40] Genesis 2:7.

imagine.[41] We, as the descendants of Adam, have the power to aspire to and achieve a better world than the one in which we currently exist.

A third meaning of "אדמה" is related to the word לדמות, "to compare". Isaiah teaches: "אֶעֱלֶה עַל־בָּמֳתֵי עָב אֶדַּמֶּה לְעֶלְיוֹן"—I will ascend above the heights of the clouds; I will be comparable to the Most High".[42] The phrase "אֶדַּמֶּה לְעֶלְיוֹן" reminds us that we, as people, should always be reaching for the ideal and striving to be Godly.

Reordering society begins by questioning the current status quo. We start the seder with the Four Questions because questions themselves bring about change and highlight the unique aspect of being human: to ask and answer.[43] By engaging in this process of discerning what is essential and true, and what is false and fantastical, our understanding of reality is transformed.

Wisdom, חכמה—*chochma*, comes from the power of questioning כֹּחַ מַה—the strength of "what?".[44] Throughout the year we strive to be *talmidei chachamim*, students and practitioners of wisdom. On the night of Passover, when we recite *Mah Nishtanah*[45]—the asking itself changes and affects change differently.

Visioning requires us to know where we are so that we can plot a path forward. We prepare for the Passover experience by searching for bread with the light of a candle, in all of the cracks and the

---

[41] Hosea 12:11.
[42] 14:14.
[43] מה and אדם have the same numerical value of 45.
[44] Mesach Chachma.
[45] The "what" is different and acts to make a difference.

crevices, to really understand our point of departure. The *seder*, meaning order, is a lesson in restoring the wholeness and equity of this broken world, as a model for a sustainable year-round version.

The wise child of the Haggadah asks: "What are the testimonies, decrees, and ordinances which Hashem, our God has commanded you?" The child wants to understand the rules, presumably so they can understand how these laws apply to the world today. The parent's answer is not about legal specificity. Instead, the answer is, "Do not eat anything after the Passover sacrifice!" We want the child to understand, and linger over, the taste of freedom. Questions are sometimes best answered by experience.

What is the taste of freedom? If we were to prepare for the needs of the world the way we prepare for the Passover seder, what would the world look like? How can we achieve it? When do we know to settle for improvements and when to start anew in pursuit of perfection? As we reflect on this time in the Jewish calendar, may we appreciate the small steps that have been taken to ameliorate oppression, but may we also be bold enough to imagine, and achieve, complete liberation.

The Spiritual Responsibility of Physical Wellbeing[46]

Judaism and Jewish texts are filled with vociferous debates and disagreements. However, nothing is more universally accepted and agreed upon than the need to protect and preserve human life and dignity. The Code of Jewish Law[47] teaches that one who even asks if it is permissible to save a life by violating Shabbat is guilty of murder. The Jerusalem Talmud[48] expresses disgust that this question could even be asked and places the blame on the local rabbi for not having made this teaching clear to everyone.

Given the enormous value that Judaism places on preserving life, the recent public mask burnings and protests are difficult to understand. The posturing of religious freedom in opposition to the

---

[46] Originally published in "Faith and Resiliency" for Torat Chayim, Winter 2021.
[47] Orach Chayim 328:2.
[48] Yoma 41b.

wellbeing of individuals and communities is blasphemy.[49] All of us must feel a religious responsibility for the safety of all people and the fidelity of our tradition. While individual spiritual practices may differ widely, our commitment to observing them safely must be unified.

We should look at the recommendations from the medical community as the minimum threshold of compliance. If social distancing is defined as "at least 6 feet apart", then 7 feet is a bigger mitzvah. Our physical well-being, and that of others, is a spiritual responsibility and must be guarded and enhanced.

The wearing of masks, frequent hand washing, and all practices that keep people healthy must be approached with the same attitude and punctiliously as any other mitzvah we seek to fulfill. In preparation for Passover we are told that we shouldn't own or eat unleavened bread.[50] We don't just remove our unleavened bread, but we prepare for days, if not weeks, cleaning, searching, and providing redundancies in the system by selling, nullifying, and burning any pieces we find.[51] We do all of this to get rid of *chametz*, and yet one must eat *chametz* on Passover, even if it is only potentially necessary to save one's life.[52]

Our rabbis remind us that we do not serve commandments, but rather the One Who Commands us, in their performance.[53] Unfortunately, we see why this warning is so necessary. By insisting on praying together in crowded spaces, in defiance of health

---

[49] Maimonides Laws of the Sabbath 2:3.
[50] Exodus 12:15–19 and 13:7.
[51] Pesachim 2a.
[52] Arukh HaShulchan, Orach Chaim 466:2.
[53] Kesef Mishnah Shabbat 2:3.

regulations, people are offering themselves and their families as sacrifices. Actually though, what God wants for us is to accept the sacrifice of having to pray alone.

So much creative thought, energy, and resources have been wasted in protest and resistance; only extending the presence of this horrific public health catastrophe. We are all frustrated that we cannot do more to quickly end this pandemic. Judaism asks that we take those feelings and invest inwardly, to think deeply about the "why", to try to understand how we might be able to change who we are, as a society, to be worthy of a different reality.

Our tradition teaches that the Temple was destroyed, and we were distanced from God's presence, because we could not get along with each other.[54] Our experience of isolation since then has been a consequence. Because we were not able to overcome baseless hatred for each other, God separates God's Self from us.

More recently, as we have been forced by Covid to distance ourselves from friends and community, we have become increasingly aware of the importance of being together. For many who have been privileged to have a place at the communal table, this isolation is newly painful. But for others, this is all they have ever known, never being seen, invited, or welcomed because of who they are. Let us do the work of building a restorative community of unity that in the merit of joining together as people, we will be able to soon come together again in person.

---

[54] Yoma 9b

Liberating Language[55]

When we become free, we need to find a new language to express that freedom. God uses four different terms of redemption to articulate the exodus from Egyptian bondage[56] and many celebrate this liberation of language by drinking four cups of wine at the seder.

It is often difficult to identify the appropriate language to capture a reordering of society. The freedoms that LGBTQ folks have achieved are all relatively recent, and the language that society uses to support these experiences is quickly changing, evolving, and approaching a more accurate representation, but there is still a lot of work left to be done.

---

[55] Originally published for the Human Rights Campaign in 2020.
[56] Exodus 6:6–7.

We celebrate new liberties with the understanding that words limit and are never as expansive as the experiences they are intended to describe. What they mean can be highly context, and person, specific. A few years ago I overheard a child ask his lesbian mother, "My friend says that when two guys like each other that means that they are gay. I know that you are gay, does that also mean that you are also a guy?"

Even more limiting than the words themselves are the construction of societal norms and definitions that accompany labels and identities. For example, if one partner in a heterosexual couple transitions, the cis partner may wonder if or how this affects their sexual orientation. A person who is bisexual may question whether committing to one exclusive partner, either male or female, conceals their identity. Genderqueer folks everywhere are failed by binary pronouns and assumptions. Feeling bound by inadequate language, just like being constrained by outdated social constructs, impedes our ability to understand and to be understood. People are obviously much more than the words that are used to represent them.

Part of the struggle is that the world has long ago established what is different by what is perceived as typical. The first of the four Passover Seder questions begins: "Why is this night different from all other nights? In response we learn that "on all other nights we eat *chametz* and matzah, but on this night only matzah." This assumes the norm that "on all other nights we eat *chametz* and matzah" when really the question being asked is "why on Passover must one only eat matzah"? Part of the re-ordering (סדר) is questioning the questions we ask and challenging the givens we are given: do we really eat *chametz* and matzah on all other nights? Are there really even four questions?

Passover represents the redemption of the soul and matzah the liberation of the body.

"Pesach", like "matzot", when it is spelled out פ"ה סמ"ך ח"ת has a numerical value of 613 which is the number of commandments, *mitzvot*, in the Torah. *Mitzvot,* when spelled out, מ"ם צד"י וא"ו תי"ו also equals 613. This teaches us that while Hebrew words in the Jewish tradition contain the essence of something, and of all that will ever exist in this world, it is also often concealed and requires effort to uncover. The tool designed for this unique work of liberating the soul, according to the *midrash*, is the heart.

The verse[57] in which God commands Moses and Aaron about the Passover sacrifice is quoted by the *midrash*:[58] "The heart alone knows its bitterness, and no outsider can share in its joy". The Meir Einei Chachamim elaborates and explains that only someone who has a heart can feel the bitterness of the soul when it is enslaved, and its elation when it is released.

Passover, *Pesach* in Hebrew, is understood as *Pe-sach*, the mouth that speaks, particularly in opposition to Pharaoh, in Hebrew—*peh ra*— the evil mouth. It is a time to bolster the dominant expression of our hearts and discover language to support the expansiveness of love.

Love is love and the Divine Heart, *lev*, contains all of the words of the entire Torah. The first and last letter of the Torah form the word "heart", but in the reverse order. Part of the work of organizing letters to form heart framed words is in sensitizing the

---

world to recognize that the love was always there, just not yet revealed.

Now, like then, language needs to be freed from the narrow constriction that confines it. With greater equality comes new opportunities and the accompanying learning curve that takes time to explore how, and what is possible. Accurate descriptions and expressions of those newfound roles and identities take even longer to manifest in verbal expression.

The four languages of redemption also correspond to the four parts of the soul: *nefesh, ruach, neshama, chayah*.[59] One's ability to speak comes from the same original Divine breath that God used to give us life.[60] The more the soul is elevated, the greater its power of speech. When we transcend the constraints of superficial labels, we will finally be able to better fulfill the mitzvah of the Haggadah; to truly tell the story of our total redemption.

---

[59] Zera Kodesh.
[60] Genesis 2:7.

The False Piety of All Lives Matter[61]

"All of the nation is holy and God dwells within each of them."[62]

Korach's argument sounds compelling. At first glance, it's not clear what he does wrong. Yet, by the middle of the *parsha*, God is so angry with Korach that he and his followers are swallowed up by the earth.

A close reading of the *parsha* reveals that Korach is a classic demagogue. His words draw people in, but his ultimate goal is his own aggrandizement. He is not seeking more power for the people, just more for himself. He convinces others to join him by alluding to a promise that God made to Israel, "You will be to Me a

---

[61] Originally published for Bayit on June 25, 2020.
[62] Numbers 16:3.

kingdom of priests and a holy nation."[63] Korach cleverly clothes his power grab in a reflection of truth.

Our rabbis teach that unless a lie begins with a little bit of truth, it will not be believed.[64] Korach crafts his words to appeal to the masses, but they are ultimately revealed to be self-serving and soulless. A similarly cynical message is being broadcast today by some in our society. They proudly proclaim, "All lives matter!" Of course, it's true, but like Korach's opening cry, it masks the speakers' actual objectives.

The appealing aspect of "All Lives Matter" is the superficial truth that of course every life is precious. But like Korach's argument, these words are said not to achieve or advance equality, but rather to abrogate responsibility to protect the lives of people of color who are continually under the threat of racial violence. Saying "All Lives Matter" falsely posits that equality has already been achieved and change is unnecessary, and implies that there is no more work to be done.

Our tradition associates a refusal to participate in collective reckoning with the behavior of a wicked child. In the Haggadah, the wicked son wants to know, "Why should I be a part of this?" He asks his parents, "What is this work for you?" as if to exclude himself from the obligation of learning about systemic racism and systems of oppression. He is not interested in anything unless it directly affects him, denying his actual connections to others.

---

[63] Exodus 19:6.
[64] Rashi, Num. 13:27.

The Hebrew words for "wicked" (רשע) and "lie" (שקר) both contain the Hebrew letter *shin*. In the mystical tradition, the letter *shin* asks God to use her to create the world.[65] God responds that since the *shin* will be misappropriated for lies, she cannot be the foundation of creation. The *shin* herself is truth, but assists in making the lie believable.

There is an old theological dispute about whether pure evil exists, or if it is simply the absence of good. The Igra D'Kala[66] posits that evil does not exist on its own. Rather, Korach took evil and attached himself to it. This is the shift from רע, potential evil, to רשע, a person who chooses to actualize it. The difference between those two words is the letter *shin*.

The Hebrew word for "truth" (אמת) comprises the Hebrew alphabet's first, middle and last letters in order, reflecting that only truth can fulfill the entire Torah.[67] By contrast, the Hebrew word for "lie" (שקר) features three of the last four letters of the alphabet with the *shin* out of order. The word "lie" literally models a distortion of reality—like Korach's distortion when he acted as though the hard work of creating meaningful change was already done.

The Ari Z"l sees Korach's claim that "All of the nation is holy and God dwells within each of them" as aspirational—and even achievable in a future time. He observes that the verse[68] for Shabbat, צדיק כתמר יפרח "a righteous person will flourish like a date

---

[65] Zohar 1:2.
[66] Rabbi Tzvi Elimelech of Dinov, 1783–1841.
[67] Ben Yehoyada on B.T. Shabbat 104a.
[68] Psalm 92.

palm", spells out Korach's name with the last letters of these three words, because in the end, Korach's claim of equal sanctity for all ultimately will be true.

In the end, when we've done the work we need to do and have built a world of complete justice and love, Korach's claim that the whole community is holy will be true. But we're not there yet.

It will only be appropriate to declare "All Lives Matter" when indeed Black, trans, and immigrant lives—when the lives of every marginalized human being—have been completely re-humanized and wholly valued. Until that time, it is a lie as old as Korach.

A Bargain at Two Zuzim

Although the narrative portion of the Haggadah starts with "This is the bread of affliction that our ancestors ate in Egypt", the story of how we originally ended up in Egypt is saved for the very last song, at the end of the Haggadah. *Chad gadya* חַד גַּדְיָא, חַד גַּדְיָא דְּזַבִּין אַבָּא בִּתְרֵי זוּזֵי, חַד גַּדְיָא, חַד גַּדְיָא—"One kid, one kid that my father bought for two *zuzim*" is understood as a reference[69] to the two goats that Jacob prepared for his father, on the night of Passover, when receiving the blessing of the first born.[70]

"Then came along the cat and ate the kid." This is referring to the jealousy that Joseph's brothers had for him and their desire to consume his birthright. It is in this maltreatment of family that both landed us in Egypt, and is perpetuating our current exile.

---

[69] See Gaon's commentary.
[70] Genesis 27:9. See Rashi there.

The brothers "took Joseph's tunic, slaughtered a kid, and dipped the tunic in the blood."[71]

We bring attention to the role the brothers played in causing pain to their father by dipping two times on the night of the seder.[72] This intergenerational trauma is passed on until the words of Joseph וְאַתֶּם עֲלוּ לְשָׁלוֹם אֶל־אֲבִיכֶם—"the rest of you go back in peace to your father"[73] is fulfilled with the Ten Martyrs, returning to our Father in Heaven.[74]

The four sons are also four brothers and the Haggadah reminds us that if we want to have a relationship with God as our parent, then we must treat all of God's children as our siblings. The Torah[75] calls this time of the year *Chodesh HaAviv*, literally the month of the father, and the Haggadah amplifies this call by distilling the evil of Lavan to אֲרַמִּי אֹבֵד אָבִי—"An Aramean tried to destroy (the concept of) my father".[76]

In the simple reading of the text, "father" is referring to our father Abraham, who represents *chesed*, acts of loving kindness. The one incident of *chesed* that is recorded,[77] tells the story of him going to invite guests while in a prophetic moment with God. As a result, the Talmud teaches[78] גְּדוֹלָה הַכְנָסַת אוֹרְחִין מֵהַקְבָּלַת פְּנֵי שְׁכִינָה—"it is better to invite guests than receiving the Divine Presence". The *Chasom Sofer* offers a parable that a parent would rather not be

---

71 Genesis 37:31.
72 See Ben Ish Chai.
73 Genesis 44:17.
74 See Rabbeinu Bachaya.
75 Exodus 23:15.
76 Deuteronomy 26:5.
77 Genesis 18:3.
78 Shabbat 127a.

invited to a family reunion, when all of the children are attending, than to go if any of them are not welcome.

It is perhaps for this reason that the Maggid begins with the story of our ancestors eating maztah in Egypt and then immediately segues into "anyone who is hungry, let them come and eat", alluding to another story that revolves around inviting guests.[79]

אַקַּמְצָא וּבַר קַמְצָא חָרוּב יְרוּשְׁלַיִם דְּהָהוּא גַּבְרָא דְּרָחֲמֵיהּ קַמְצָא וּבְעֵל דְּבָבֵיהּ
בַּר קַמְצָא עֲבַד סְעוֹדָתָא אֲמַר לֵיהּ לְשַׁמָּעֵיהּ זִיל אַיְיתִי לִי קַמְצָא אֲזַל אַיְיתִי
לֵיהּ בַּר קַמְצָא

The Gemara explains: Jerusalem was destroyed on account of Kamtza and bar Kamtza. This is as there was a certain man whose friend was named Kamtza and whose enemy was named bar Kamtza. He once made a large feast and said to his servant: Go bring me my friend Kamtza. The servant went and mistakenly brought him his enemy bar Kamtza."

The Maharsha comments that it is possible that Kamtza is actually bar Kamtza's father, providing greater context into the personal nature of blatant hatred. Every interaction between people is also an interaction with God. Even if the brothers didn't like Joseph, their knowledge of how it would affect their father Jacob, should have informed their actions.

This also motivates why we read about the role of Elijah the Prophet on Shabbat Hagadol. We center the cup of Elijah, and

---

[79] Gittin 55b.

open the door for him, to bring attention to our desire to make peace with one another.[80]

וְהֵשִׁיב לֵב־אָבוֹת עַל־בָּנִים וְלֵב בָּנִים עַל־אֲבוֹתָם פֶּן־אָבוֹא וְהִכֵּיתִי אֶת־הָאָרֶץ חֵרֶם הנה אנכי שולח לכם את אליה הנביא לפני בוא יום יהוה הגדול והנורא—"He shall reconcile parents with children and children with their parents, so that, when I come, I do not strike the whole land with utter destruction."

It doesn't cost a lot to be nice to each other, and being healed from the inherited trauma of it all is priceless. The only way that we can have an unbroken home, in Jerusalem, is when we start treating each other as healthy families should.

---

[80] Malachi 3:24.

Iyar

A Second Chance for Accessibility[81]

Pesach Sheni acknowledges that changing the date, but not the criteria for admittance, doesn't solve for those whose condition doesn't shift with the calendar. Truly expanding from a posture of exclusion to inclusion is difficult as a response after the fact. An important aspect of this holiday is to reflect on how the ideal wasn't achieved, so that next year we can get it right the first time.

God's creation of the world was thoughtfully intentional. On Friday evenings, as we welcome Shabbat we sing: מֵרֹאשׁ מִקֶּדֶם נְסוּכָה. סוֹף מַעֲשֶׂה בְּמַחֲשָׁבָה תְּחִלָּה—"Shabbat was anointed from the outset. Last to be created, Shabbat was first in God's mind."

---

[81] Originally published for Bayit on May 17, 2022.

God's meticulous design of all of creation challenges us to be deliberate and careful in our own planning. Whether in our preparations for shabbat or organizing for Jewish communal events, the calculated construction of the world and the intricacies of Jewish laws remind us to take all possibilities into account as we arrange sacred spaces. The beautiful vision we imagine for our communities will only be achieved with careful forethought— *machshava techila*—to ensure that accessibility for all people won't be an afterthought.

While properly preparing increases the likelihood of a successful outcome, it is rarely guaranteed. The possibility of the unexpected, or things that are simply beyond our control, is part of the human experience. Judaism recognizes that life happens. The last two years have demonstrated, more powerfully than we could have expected, that we are not in control of everything.

The Talmud introduces the principle of אונס רחמנא פטרי "The Merciful One" exempts those whose circumstances are beyond their control.[82] Even in situations where we have the agency to make choices, it can be difficult to prioritize between competing interests. The Gemara in Sukkah teaches the concept of הָעוֹסֵק בְּמִצְוָה פָּטוּר מִן הַמִּצְוָה: one who is engaged in a mitzvah is exempt from [the other] mitzvah. Knowing that it is impossible for human beings to fully anticipate all the circumstances of life, and knowing that the sheer number of mitzvot and important tasks to accomplish can be easily overwhelming, God enables us to focus on the mitzvah of the moment rather than stressing about whatever it is we are not accomplishing at the same time.

---

[82] Nedarim 27a.

Rabbi Yosei HaGelili teaches that this principle was learned from those who carried Joseph's casket out of Egypt. Because they were impure from contact with a corpse, they were unable to offer the Passover sacrifice. But, since they were performing the mitzvah of caring for the deceased, they were exempt from the mitzvah of bringing the paschal lamb.

However, being told that they were excluded from the responsibility, because it wasn't for people in their state of being, did nothing to offer comfort. Instead, they ask Moses, לָ֥מָּה נִגָּרַ֖ע—"why should we be left out?".[83] God didn't respond with the previous axiom of exemption, but answers with a new opportunity and holiday:

דַּבֵּ֛ר אֶל־בְּנֵ֥י יִשְׂרָאֵ֖ל לֵאמֹ֑ר אִ֣ישׁ אִ֣ישׁ כִּי־יִהְיֶֽה־טָמֵ֣א ׀ לָנֶ֗פֶשׁ או֜ בְדֶ֣רֶךְ רְחֹקָה֩ לָכֶ֗ם א֚וֹ לְדֹרֹ֣תֵיכֶ֔ם וְעָ֥שָׂה פֶ֖סַח לַיהוָֽה׃

Speak to the Israelite people, saying: When any party—whether you or your posterity—who is defiled by a corpse or is on a long journey, they may still offer a sacrifice to Hashem.

This sacrifice is brought one month later, on the 14th of Iyar, known as Pesach Sheni. The law is established not just for that generation, but for every generation. Not just for those who are

---

impure, but for anyone who finds themselves at a distance[84] from where they want to be.[85]

Joseph is central to the story of Passover.[86] It is because his brothers sell him into slavery in Egypt that the rest of the family eventually comes to Egypt and is enslaved there until the Exodus. Joseph wanted to be close to his brothers but they rejected him and sent him far away. They see him approaching "from a distance, and before he came close to them they conspired to kill him"— וַיִּרְאוּ אֹתוֹ מֵרָחֹק וּבְטֶרֶם יִקְרַב אֲלֵיהֶם וַיִּתְנַכְּלוּ אֹתוֹ לַהֲמִיתוֹ.[87]

In Pesachim[88] we are taught: "וָיו מוֹסִיף". The letter *vuv*, which shares its name with the hooks[89] in the Tabernacle that connected the curtains to the pillars, is a conjunction and adds, just as Joseph's name means to increase.[90] The additional Passover, originating for those who made sure that Joseph wasn't left behind,[91] asks us to arrange our lives not around the convenience of doing our own mitzvot and achieving our own goals, but also around accommodating the needs of others. This month of Iyar[92] which

---

84 Rashi observes the dot over the word רְחֹקָה—"distant" to mean not literally geographically.

85 Rokeach observes that רחוקה = חוץ למקום.

86 The custom of dipping at the seder is widely understood to be referencing his coat that was dipped in blood.

87 Genesis 37:18.

88 5a.

89 Exodus 38:19.

90 Genesis 30:24.

91 Bal Haturim אנשים אשר היו טמאים לנפש אדם בגימ' אלו שהיו נושאין ארונו של יוסף.

92 The "ר" of אייר stands for Rachel, Joseph's mother, who is buried on the way to comfort those who are distanced and transmitted signs so her sister, Leah, could be with Jacob.

corresponds, in the mystical tradition,[93] to thoughtfulness (הרהור) and is governed by the letter *vuv*, invites us to expand how we think about interacting and connecting with each other.

In the spiritual world, a person can be physically close, but spiritually distant. The opposite is also true. God is always accessible—those who were excluded called out "לָמָּה נִגָּרֵע"— because they knew God was listening. The desire to be in connection is what created this mitzvah. Providing appropriate access is part of the purification process our institutions desperately need.

In our imperfect world, only the Divine is capable of perfection. The messiness and fragility of human life means that mistakes are inevitable for all of us. When we are caught up in ensuring our own perfect experiences, keeping ourselves occupied and undistracted for the sake of our own goals, we neglect the needs of those around us and ignore the realities of our world.

Connecting these needs with our resources is a holy communal act of transcendence where the physical is repurposed for the spiritual. Making sure that folks who use a wheelchair, are genderqueer, or those who are genderqueer and use a wheelchair, have safe access to bathrooms is just as sacred as our belief in the holiness of God's creations. Just as providing English translations on source sheets is a standard practice, we should also ensure that ASL, braille, or an oral accompaniment of the text is available as well.

A letter *vuv* models a "Yes. And…" mentality. The timing of this holiday reminds us to take advantage of the opportunity that God

---

[93] Sefer Yetzirah 5:7.

gives to plan and plan again, supporting an awareness that there is always more we can be doing.

Allied for Torah[94]

The Torah begins with the letter *bet*, the second letter of the Hebrew Alphabet, and concludes with the letter *lamed*, a language of learning (the word for "learn" is "*lamed*—למד", the same letters that form the letter "ל"), because learning Torah is intended to be done with another person. The Talmud teaches that the Torah is only acquired *b'chabura*, within a collective:[95]

לְפִי שֶׁאֵין הַתּוֹרָה נִקְנֵית אֶלָּא בַּחֲבוּרָה. כִּדְרַבִּי יוֹסֵי בְּרַבִּי חֲנִינָא, דְּאָמַר רַבִּי יוֹסֵי בְּרַבִּי חֲנִינָא: מַאי דִּכְתִיב "חֶרֶב אֶל הַבַּדִּים וְנֹאָלוּ"—חֶרֶב עַל שׂוֹנְאֵיהֶם שֶׁל תַּלְמִידֵי חֲכָמִים שֶׁיוֹשְׁבִים בַּד בְּבַד וְעוֹסְקִים בַּתּוֹרָה.

Expounding on the verse in Jeremiah,[96] they continue homiletically: **A sword upon the enemies of Torah scholars,**

---

[94] Originally published in *Chaver Up!* April 2021.
[95] Bavli Berachot 63b.
[96] 50:36.

a euphemism for the Torah scholars themselves, **who sit alone and study Torah.**

Being in relationship with the community is a condition for learning Torah today, just as it was a prerequisite for the giving of the Torah at Mount Sinai—"ויחן שם ישראל נגד ההר"—Israel (singular) encamped opposite the mountain".[97] In Derech Eretz Zuta, we find an interesting explanation for the specific timing of this epic event: "God said since they have made themselves one encampment (*chania*), the time has come to give them my Torah." The Or Hachaim[98] explains that the gathering was not a collection of separate individuals showing up together, at the same time and place, but was a unification of the people, coming together to complement and complete (ויחן) "Like one person with one heart".[99]

We find a similar language describing the Egyptians chasing after the Israelites,[100] but the order is reversed: "With one heart, like one person".[101] A common goal and focus can organize people, but they remain distinct and disjointed.[102] Coming together for a purpose is not the same as coming together as a person.

Allyship is often seen as a response by someone of privilege, or with resources, to the oppression or affliction of another. This is only necessary when the unity of our humanity breaks down. The

---

[97] Exodus 19:2.
[98] Exodus 19:3.
[99] Mechilta.
[100] Exodus 14:10.
[101] Rashi.
[102] Pachad Yitzchak.

more ideal model is where people are as connected to each other as they are to themselves. We wouldn't then need a commitment to "create safe spaces", or even to dismantle unsafe spaces, because we never would have allowed them to exist at all.

Torah, when studied properly together, protects us, and preempts the need for systemic change because it gives everyone an immediate awareness of the needs and experiences of each other. It even defends against outside forces that come to challenge our peaceful coexistence. When Sennacherib came to destroy Jerusalem, King Hezekiah **"inserted a sword at the entrance of the study hall and said: Anyone who does not engage in studying Torah shall be stabbed with this sword."**[103]

מה עשה נעץ חרב על פתח בית המדרש ואמר כל מי שאינו עוסק בתורה ידקר בחרב זו.

The word for "sword—חרב", and "ally—חבר", are the same three letters, just in a different order. "Sennacherib—סנחריב", is understood as an anagram for "The prince of the sword", חרב נסי.[104] This is an allusion to the blessing that Esav received "By your sword shall you live" [105] and the tradition that if the voice, קול, of Jacob is found in the study halls[106] then the hands of Esav won't be able to be destructive.[107]

---

103 Bavli Sanhedrin 94b.
104 Ben Yehyada.
105 Genesis 27:40.
106 In the verse Genesis 27:22, the word "voice" is repeated as an allusion to the necessity of having multiple voices in Torah study (B.Y. Taanit 7a).
107 Eicha Rabbah.

The numerical value of "voice—קול" and "study—למד" together equal "חבר—ally". Our need to learn together, as the way to acquire Torah is further alluded to in the word "*chabura*", collective—חבורה, which is the same word as "חבר", just with an additional ו and ה.[108] The *vuv* represents the six orders of the Mishnah, and the *hey* alludes to the five books of the Torah.

At the time of the giving of the Torah, allies were not needed because everything was perfect. Receiving the Torah at Mount Sinai healed the brokenness of the world. The *midrash*[109] says that there were no illnesses or ailments. All needs were provided for, and each person was whole. It was also the first time, since the Garden of Eden, that the world was safe again for God to come out, as God's Self.

The blatant hatred to those whom we perceive as "other", institutionalized and mass produced by systems that oppress and dehumanize, has forced God back into the closet. Allyship is the recognition that we have inherited a broken world, and it is on us to fix it.

It is also a model of restorative religion. The Baal Haturim[110] describes the two cherubs on the ark "like two chaverim engaged in the back and forth of learning Torah". The Sforno adds "their wings [spread] in an upward direction, as if reflecting that they had received spiritual inspiration (from the contents of the ark) enabling them to fly".

---

[108] Ben Yehyada Brachot 63.
[109] Mekhilta Exodus 20.
[110] Exodus 25:18.

Elevation over subjugation is the path necessary to gain entrance to sacred spaces. After humans were banished from the Garden of Eden, God placed the "cherubim and revolving sword, to guard the way to the tree of life"[111] and continues to deny entry to those who try and limit the access of others.[112]

When we learn about, and with, those of a different lived experience, we expand our understanding of the Torah and fulfill its purpose in elevating humanity. We must come together, for God, Torah, and each other.

---

[111] Genesis 3:24.
[112] See Tuyul B'Pardes p.297.

Counting on Community to End AIDS[113]

Advances in the treatment, prevention, and de-stigmatization of HIV/AIDS have improved dramatically over the past several decades. But the AIDS walk in New York City this Sunday reminds us that we still have a great distance to go to end AIDS in New York by 2020, in the United States by 2025, and worldwide by 2030.

This year, the AIDS walk falls during Sefirat HaOmer, the 49 days that Jews count between the festivals of Passover and Shavuot, and just before Lag Ba'Omer, the 33rd day in this counting. This seven-week period marks the time between the exodus from Egypt and receiving the Torah at Sinai.

This window of time is a period of semi-mourning on the Jewish calendar. We remember a different epidemic that occurred in

---

[113] Originally published on May 17, 2019 and co-authored with Seth Marnin.

Talmudic times. The Talmud teaches that it was during this exact time of the year, in the second century, that 24,000 students of Rabbi Akiva, one of the greatest scholars of the Mishnah, died in a terrible plague. We learn that the students suffered because "they did not treat each other with respect".[114] That many people dying is a devastating loss of biblical proportions.[115]

Next week, on Lag Ba'Omer, we commemorate and celebrate the end of that plague. According to tradition, the plague ended on the 33rd day of the Omer. (The Hebrew letters *lamed* and *gimel* which make up the acronym "Lag" have the combined numerical value of 33.) Our rabbis teach that the plague ended only because R' Akiva's most important lesson, to "love your neighbors like [you love] yourself" was finally learned. As a result, Lag Ba'Omer became a happy day, interrupting the sad-ness of the Omer period for twenty-four hours.

According to the Center for Disease Control and Prevention (CDC), in 2017 (the most recent year for which this information is available), the number of new HIV diagnoses in the United States was still more than 38,700. An estimated 1.1 million people in the United States were living with HIV at the end of 2016. Of those people, about 14%, or 1 in 7, did not know they had HIV. It is estimated that 692,790 Americans have died of HIV-related illnesses since the start of the pandemic in 1982.

Although there is much work to be done to combat AIDS, we have learned many things since the beginning of the pandemic. We now know that antiretroviral medications can sustain the health of

---

[114] Yevamos 62b.
[115] Numbers 25:9.

people living with HIV and stop transmission of HIV to others. We know that we must expand access to healthcare, ensure comprehensive sexual health education and services, and increase access to preventative measures like pre-exposure prophylaxis (PrEP). And we know that people living with HIV who have an undetectable level of the virus in their blood through effective treatment cannot pass the virus on to others.

While the numbers may feel overwhelming, organizations like Housing Works and GMHC continue to work tirelessly to prevent HIV/AIDS transmission, provide care, and advocate to end AIDS. Perhaps just as importantly, these organizations—and so many others—have worked to end the stigma surrounding HIV/AIDS.

Our Rabbis explain that during the Omer we mourn the loss of those 24,000 who died because they failed to treat each other with dignity. We are constantly reminded that as a community, we have still not sufficiently internalized the mandate of treating each other—or ourselves—with respect. Self-care includes getting tested, knowing our status, having accurate information, ensuring that resources are accessible, and ending the stigma.

As we count the days of the Omer, we recall the ending of the plague of the second century and prepare to receive and accept the Torah at Sinai. Let us also acknowledge our communal responsibility to respect each other and ensure that we end this modern-day plague too.

Building Sacred Spaces[116]

Jewish tradition teaches that God is constantly recreating this world, building something out of nothing. The fact that we are here right now testifies, in this very moment, to God's intention for us to be here.

By contrast, when we build something, we are simply making something out of something else. We are really just taking things that have already existed—like trees, stones, and other elements—and changing their form into buildings and furniture. As a result, we can move away from our creations, and they continue to exist without us. However, if God were to stop thinking about us for even a second, we would cease to exist like we were never here.

---

[116] Originally published for Bayit on February 10, 2019.

In this week's *parsha*, *Tetzaveh*, we read,[117]

וְשָׁכַנְתִּי בְּתוֹךְ בְּנֵי יִשְׂרָאֵל וְהָיִיתִי לָהֶם לֵאלֹהִים: וְיָדְעוּ כִּי אֲנִי יְהוָה אֱלֹהֵיהֶם
אֲשֶׁר הוֹצֵאתִי אֹתָם מֵאֶרֶץ מִצְרַיִם לְשָׁכְנִי בְתוֹכָם אֲנִי יְהוָה אֱלֹהֵיהֶם:

I will abide among the Israelites, and I will be their God. And
they shall know that I, Adonai, am their God, who brought
them out from the land of Egypt that I might abide among
them, I, Adonai, their God.

Everything we do in Jewish life comes with this reminder: God
dwells within and among us. We build a space for God in order to
be reminded who freed us from the narrow place, and who liberates
us even now.

God is continually building this world for us. In return, we're called
to reciprocate places for God as reminders of the One who releases
us from constriction. When we build those places, it is essential that
we truly accommodate the needs of God's creations.

There is a beautiful *midrash* about the construction of the portable
sanctuary, the *mishkan*. The Rabbis imagine a king who has only one
daughter, and that daughter marries a king from another land. After
some time the son-in-law wants to return home with his bride.

The father explains to the younger king, "I understand that you
want to go home, and I can't tell you not to take my daughter with
you—she's your wife! But she's my only daughter, and I can't bear

---

[117] Exodus 29:45–46.

to be separated from her. Rather, please do me this favor: wherever you go, make guest quarters for me so that I can dwell with you."

So too God said to Israel, "I've given you the Torah. I can't tell you not to take it—it's yours now. But I can't bear to be separated from it. Rather, every place that you go, make me a home where I can live. As it is said: 'Build for Me a sanctuary'…"

The Zohar expands "sanctuary" beyond just the *mishkan* to mean any sacred space. "How beloved are we by God that in every place where we are found, God's presence is among us, as it says, 'build for me a sanctuary and I will dwell among them;' all spaces where people gather are called a sanctuary."

Often the spaces where we gather aren't really sanctuaries, though. They may not be accessible on a physical level. And even when they are ADA-compliant, they may exclude people for emotional, intellectual, and/or spiritual reasons. Too often, some of God's children are excluded, unwelcomed, and suppressed—often in the false name of making these spaces "welcoming" for God.

The Talmud teaches that "It is greater to invite guests than it is to greet the Divine Presence." Welcoming each other, in all that we are, is more important even than welcoming God's own Presence into our midst! The tradition teaches that God is like a Parent who experiences pleasure when their children get along, not when we create ostensibly "God-focused" events while excluding any of God's children… whether that means excluding people on the basis of gender expression or sexual orientation, or on the basis of race, or because of what form of denominational Judaism they practice.

Indeed, excluding each other from community is a form of the senseless hatred that caused God's Temple to be destroyed 2,000 years ago.[118] The Talmud[119] teaches that although God no longer (since the Temple's destruction) has a physical address, we can still seek and find God in the four cubits of *halachah*, Jewish law. We can still seek and find God in the open space that's contained within the scaffolding of tradition, law, and interpretation.

Last week's Torah portion called us to build a sanctuary for God, that God might dwell within and among us. This week's Torah portion links that building with our core story of liberation, reminding us that we must build our holy spaces, both literal and metaphorical. As we build the Jewish future, it must be with a constant remembrance of the One Who brings us forth from narrow places.

Torah offers us Divine specifications for supporting sacred space, and when we follow those instructions we become co-creators with God. God builds the world for us, and in return we build holy space for God. God liberates us from Egypt, and in return we are called to liberate others from small-mindedness and exclusion.

The holy support that we provide our communities requires our renewed and constant involvement, just like God continuously reinvests in keeping the world in existence. We must expand and reconfigure our sanctuaries to protect, inspire, and nourish the evolving needs of the Jewish people. If we don't, then God won't have the space to live among us.

---

[118] Yoma 9b.
[119] Brachos 8a.

Sivan

Embracing LGBTQ Jews for Shavuot[120]

The Torah was never given to an individual, but rather to a nation. For far too long, many communities have forced those who come out—to get out. As a result, we—and the Torah we study—are deficient. Our rabbis teach that if we want to properly accept the Torah on Shavuot, we need to accept it as we originally did: with complete unity and acceptance of each other. That means that we must proactively engage our queer siblings and refocus our communal responsibility to ensure queer folks can be out—while staying in religious spaces.

It is perhaps for this reason that the Code of Jewish Law instructs us to read the *parsha* of Bamidbar before Shavuot.[121] Bamidbar

---

[120] Originally published for Bayit on June 2, 2022.
[121] Orach Chayim 428:4.

begins with taking a census of the whole congregation of Israel "שְׂאוּ אֶת־רֹאשׁ כָּל־עֲדַת בְּנֵי־יִשְׂרָאֵל".[122] This was done by each person contributing a half shekel, which reminds us that by ourselves we are incomplete, and we need the other to be whole.[123]

Being gay or trans isn't a choice; but being homophobic or transphobic is. Like we chose to accept the Torah, we must also choose to accept those to whom the Torah is given. Loving others like we love ourselves,[124] is an important principle of [obtaining] Torah and it takes a lot of effort to overcome the cultural norms of discrimination.[125]

Loving people—אוֹהֵב אֶת הַבְּרִיּוֹת—is one of the 48 ways of acquiring Torah[126] because through this love, one puts themselves back into the collective. Only then is one fitting to receive the Torah, which was given to the collective.[127] The Maharal testifies to the opposite as well: "If someone doesn't love others, they are separating themselves from the *klal* and won't merit Torah". When we exclude others we are actually removing ourselves.

Shavuot is a celebration of acceptance, and so too is Pride. The absence of embracing is an act of severance. Like righteousness, inclusion is something that we must pursue—רדף. We run after that which we want to be one with and not reaching out to folks that have been marginalized is an additional act of פרד—separation.[128]

---

[122] Numbers 1:2.
[123] R' Shlomo Alkebetz.
[124] Leviticus 19:18.
[125] Toras Kohanim 4:12.
[126] Pirkei Avos 6:5.
[127] Derech Chaim.
[128] These two words, "*perud*" and "*rodeph*" have the same three letters in Hebrew.

Our souls all have a shared source,[129] and in the spiritual world there can be no interruption between them. Loving peace—שלום requires seeking out those who are in need of it, and healing the unnatural divisiveness that caused the lack of completion—שלם. It was only when we were like one person, with one heart, that God said, "the time has come for Me to give the Torah".[130]

The Rabbis[131] apply this dynamic today as well: "Anyone who isn't a guarantor, and at one with the people to whom they are teaching Torah, shouldn't teach them". *Midrash Tanchuma*[132] takes it even further:

אָסוּר לְתַלְמִיד חָכָם לְהוֹרוֹת הֲלָכָה בַּצִּבּוּר, עַד שֶׁיְּהוּ דִּבְרֵי תוֹרָה עֲרֵבִין עַל שׁוֹמְעֵיהֶם, כַּכַּלָּה הַזוֹ שֶׁהִיא עֲרֵבָה עַל בַּעְלָהּ וּמִתְאַוֶּה לִהְיוֹת שׁוֹמֵעַ אֶת דְּבָרֶיהָ.

It is forbidden for a Torah scholar to teach Jewish Law to a congregation until their words are pleasant and unified to those who are listening, like a bride whose words are desired by her partner.

A variation of this teaching explains the parable of a bride in the context of וַיִּתֵּן אֶל מֹשֶׁה כְּכַלֹּתוֹ—when we were given the Torah we were beloved as a bride. The sweetness that is achieved in our relationships with God, Torah, and people, is dependent on our closeness and understanding of the other. This is part of the

---

[129] See שער הגלגולים הקדמה יז.
[130] Midrash Leviticus Rabbah 9:9.
[131] Shir Hashirim Rabbah.
[132] Ki Tisa 16:2.

blessing over the Torah that one makes every morning—נא והערב, "please sweeten"—which is born out of Moses' love for the people.[133]

Shavuot is *Zman Matan Torateinu*—זְמַן מַתַּן תּוֹרָתֵינוּ—the time of our receiving God's Torah. As we prepare to celebrate Shavuot, we must again make a choice—בחר: do we want to ally and attach ourselves to the *klal*—חבר, or will we be the ones running away—ברח—from our covenantal responsibility?

---

[133] Tiferet Shlomo.

Rabbi Mike Moskowitz

Allyship is Not in Heaven[134]

At this epic moment in our lives, many people are understanding for the first time the need to be active in the holy resistance against racism. For those of us who are privileged to live without the fear of racial violence, we want to be involved and fight for change but often worry about how to best ally with communities of color.

Some are concerned about getting it "wrong" even as we know that there is no one right way to be an ally. Delivering that pure intentionality to the world of action is a sensitive balance. What may be validating and affirming for one person, or in one situation, might be traumatic and offensive with another.

Allyship can feel awkward. It is hard work—sometimes uncomfortable and painful—not just because it is predicated on

---

[134] Originally published for *The Times of Israel* Blog, on June 11, 2020 and co-authored with Seth Marnin.

people being dehumanized but also because we recognize our own complicity in it. Being an ally requires an exceptional precision to take up the appropriate amount of space. That exactness can be as aspirational as it may be elusive, even for seasoned allies.

But allyship, like Torah, is not "beyond reach." It is accessible to us all. The Torah tells us about itself:

לֹא בַשָּׁמַיִם הִוא לֵאמֹר מִי יַעֲלֶה־לָּנוּ הַשָּׁמַיְמָה וְיִקָּחֶהָ לָּנוּ וְיַשְׁמִעֵנוּ אֹתָהּ
וְנַעֲשֶׂנָּה: וְלֹא־מֵעֵבֶר לַיָּם הִוא לֵאמֹר מִי יַעֲבָר־לָנוּ אֶל־עֵבֶר הַיָּם וְיִקָּחֶהָ לָּנוּ
וְיַשְׁמִעֵנוּ אֹתָהּ וְנַעֲשֶׂנָּה: כִּי־קָרוֹב אֵלֶיךָ הַדָּבָר מְאֹד בְּפִיךָ וּבִלְבָבְךָ לַעֲשֹׂתוֹ:

"[Torah] is not in the heavens, that you should say, 'Who among us can go up to the heavens and get it for us and impart it to us, that we may observe it?' Neither is it beyond the sea, that you should say, 'Who among us can cross to the other side of the sea and get it for us and impart it to us, that we may observe it?' No, the thing is very close to you, in your mouth and in your heart, to observe it."[135]

Accessing allyship, like Torah, is incremental, a long-term commitment, and requires a lot of work. A Rebbe of mine[136] observed that it is odd for the Torah to offer this navigational assistance. How is it that a person could think the Torah is so far away—in Heaven or across the sea—when it is actually so near at hand that it is literally in our mouths and hearts?

---

[135] Deuteronomy 30:12–14.
[136] Rav Helman of the Mir.

The *midrash*[137] explains by giving us an example of two people who enter the study hall. The foolish one says "There is too much to learn! It is a mixture of Hebrew and Aramaic. There is no capitalization and no punctuation. I'm never going to be able to finish it!" And so they leave and refuse to learn anything. The wise one says: "There is a lot to learn. However, I can learn two teachings today. Another two tomorrow. And over time, I will learn the entire Torah."

The world is broken. Tradition tells us that the best way to cope with the brokenness and fear is to engage and try to fix it. There is no shortage of injustices to protest, letters to write, lessons to learn, and voices to hear. It can feel overwhelming and, like the fool, one could give up without even trying. Or, like the wise one, we can envision how over time our collective efforts, as imperfect or insignificant as they may feel today, can bring about a perfected future.

As our Rabbis teach, "No one can do everything, but everyone can do something."[138] We each have something unique to offer. The more we learn about allyship, the more informed our personal response can be. What is one chapter of allyship we can learn today?

---

[137] Vayikrah Rabbah.
[138] Heard many times from Rabbi Kleinbaum.

Coming Out Against Hate[139]

This weekend we celebrate, with pride, God's "coming out" speech—the Divine Revelation at Mount Sinai. Our need to be seen and understood for who we are has its source in the Divine's perfection and identity as a giver.[140]

The Jewish community and LGBTQ community share long experiences of being closeted, forced—in different ways—to choose between being unsafe or hiding the fullness of who we are. Moving about the world as someone recognizably Jewish, or LGBTQ, or both, has often meant being subject to hate, discrimination, and attack.

---

[139] Originally published for Bayit on June 7, 2019 and co-authored with Rabbi Marisa James.
[140] See Ramchal in Derech HaShem.

For centuries Jewish life, and perhaps all spiritual life, was built within closets. As we felt the need to hide the fullness of our truest selves, we built hiding spaces in society and religion out of fear.

But that's not the Judaism, or the world that we are called to build. We are instructed to construct a world that reflects and uplifts the many diversities of God's splendor, the many colors of the rainbow refracting God's infinite light.

To create that world, first we must be honest with ourselves about how much work still lies ahead, and who must do it. Many who grew up in America over the last 50 years believed that anti-Semitism had become far more an historical relic than a modern reality. Many LGBTQ people and allies, especially over the last decade, thought that progress was flourishing: legal protections were expanding rapidly, and civic leaders increasingly took our safety and health seriously.

But Dr. Martin Luther King's prophetic vision of an ever more just and inclusive world—while ultimately true on God's timeline, isn't automatically true on ours. The arc of the moral universe doesn't automatically bend toward justice. We must bend it that way.

Today, societal forces are mounting to undo the progress of the last several decades—targeting houses of worship, inciting fear and hate, shoving whole communities back into closets that we thought were long outdated.

The good news is that we are not alone. We are not building alone, and as always, we are far stronger together than any of us could ever be on our own. Advancements against anti-Semitism and homophobia have always been incremental and cooperative. Progress happens slowly, and requires the collaboration of many to produce a future that has everyone in mind.

It's easy to focus on building a world that is better "for us"—forgetting that the only way to truly make that better world is to build it for all. How many cisgender white gays and lesbians celebrated when marriage equality became a reality, but were absent from ongoing activism for their trans siblings? How many progressive Jews felt that anti-Semitism had vanished from their lives, not noticing that our visibly Jewish Orthodox siblings faced continued attacks? How many white Jews are activists on behalf of Jews of color? It goes on and on.

Real progress means expanding beyond our own communities and specific interests. The fact that many of us have yet experienced certain vulnerabilities and inequalities does not mean that we are protected from them. The privileges that shield us today can easily slip away tomorrow, God forbid. But as history keeps teaching, if we don't stand up for others, there won't be anyone left to stand up for us.

This ongoing work is both external and internal. We need to build outward and advocate for others,[141] while at the same time, building inward and strengthening connections that nurture and nourish each other.

Now, 50 years since Stonewall, this work is far from complete. To paraphrase the charge given at *b'nei mitzvah* celebrations: this must not be the end of our activism, but the beginning. In the words of our sages, although it is not on us to "complete" this work, neither are we free to refrain from it.

---

[141] For instance, straight and cisgender allies must advocate for the LGBTQ community, and non-Jewish allies must stand up for the Jewish community.

This year's Pride Month coincides with Shavuot, the end of Judaism's seven-week cycle of counting the *Omer*, moving from the Exodus story, to the receiving of the Torah. Over these 49 days, we followed the example of the Children of Israel in the desert, working to transform ourselves from a newly freed mixed multitude into a unified humanity able to stand together at Sinai and receive the holy Torah. During this time, we reaffirm our spiritual duty to ensure that all are protected and safe, so that we all can stand together as one.

Unity is core to Jewish spiritual life. Tradition teaches that we received the Torah only as a cohesive community, with each and every person equally invited, present, and welcomed. The completeness of Torah depended on the wholeness of community. The Torah scroll is not considered kosher with even one letter missing. So too, a community with even one person excluded or dehumanized cannot ever be a truly holy community.

There are significant spiritual consequences if anyone feels pressured to conceal who they really are, especially if it is out of a fear of not being fully accepted. In that same spirit, the Revelation at Sinai was a true Divine "coming out" to the world. What little our enslaved ancestors knew about God was in their liberation from bondage. But now, God would reveal God's Self. God's "I" narrative of introduction at Sinai reminds us that there is but one God, in whose image we all are created.[142] To discriminate against a person, for just being, is to discriminate against the Source of all being.

---

[142] Exodus 20:1–2.

On Shavuot, we remember the moment when God said, "This is who I Am". God's identity needs no affirmation, but God still gave humanity the opportunity to say, "Yes, we see You, and we will call You by the names You teach us." God modeled coming out, and God modeled how we should treat everyone.

This Shavuot and Pride Month, may we all continue the work and blessing of ongoing Revelation. Accepting the Torah is predicated on us accepting each other. Building a future, without closets of fear, requires fully seeing each other and being completely present as ourselves.

What Shavuot Teaches Us About #MeToo[143]

"When someone shows you who they are, believe them the
first time."
—Maya Angelou

As we approach Shavuot, we recognize the parallels between the revelation at Sinai and the #MeToo Movement. What lessons can we learn from our experience at Sinai that we can use to mitigate the damaging effects of toxic masculinity?

When God revealed God's Self at Sinai, it wasn't the first time God tried to be recognized. In the beginning, we are told, it was with ten soft utterances that God spoke this world into existence. That is, from the very beginning, God wanted us to see God in the

---

[143] Originally published for *The Times of Israel* Blog on June 6, 2019 and co-authored with Seth Marnin.

beautiful simplicity of this complex world. God, you could say, was being subtle.

When God created the world, in the Genesis narrative, God's name אלוקים "Elokim" is used. The name אלוקים alludes to God's hiddenness and can be parsed to mean מי אלה—"Whose is this?", or "To whom does this world belong?". It also has the same numerical value as the word for nature, הטבע. God wanted us to recognize the beauty of the world and ask who created it? God also wanted us to see, hear, and understand God. To be in relationship with God. But we were not so astute, and over and over humanity failed.

So too with the #MeToo Movement. Decades (indeed centuries!) before Tarana Burke launched the #MeToo Movement, women and girls spoke both softly and loudly. But, not so unlike the frustrations and outrage God experienced, they were often doubted, ignored, rejected, and went unheard. Toxic masculinity throughout the ages has damaged both women and men, rendering us unrecognizable, as people, to each other and to God.

It is sometimes challenging to learn something new but it is incredibly difficult to unknow it once you learn it. And it isn't always easy to know what to do with that knowledge once you acquire it. But we cannot look away either. We are responsible for acting with the information we have access to. It may not be easy, but we are obligated.

There were always individuals, like Abraham, who were sensitive to the awkward privilege of existing in a world that was created by another. So they searched until they found God, meaning, and purpose. The broader society, however, didn't hear God's call for human dignity and it was only through the death and destruction of the Ten Plagues in Egypt that God was finely revealed to the world with a harsher Ten Commandments.

God gave the Torah to Moses and the Jewish people on Mount Sinai. We are each meant to toil every day to try to understand what our unique responsibility in our relationship with God is, with the Torah containing the details of that relationship.

There has been a similar struggle in our awareness of toxic masculinity. There have always been people who have recognized it, and its consequences, and tried to combat it. And, as there has been a recent communal revelation in naming at least some of the manifestations of the problem, we all now must be held responsible. And we all, especially men, must toil every day to understand our responsibility in relationship to women, girls, and nonbinary people.

Rashi writes that God presents as the groom, in the marriage to the Jewish people, at Mount Sinai. God asked us if we were interested in the Torah. We answered with enthusiastic consent.

When we say Kiddush on Friday night, the day of the week that the Torah was originally given, we say that it is a remembrance both of the exodus out of Egypt and the creation of the world—זֵכֶר לִיצִיאַת מִצְרָיִם...זִכָּרוֹן לְמַעֲשֵׂה בְרֵאשִׁית. Although no one was there to witness the beginning of God creating the world, the Divine Revelation, and miracles in Egypt, provide a rational basis to believe God's Genesis story. We are all capable of believing that something happened, even when we were not there to actually witness it.

What might it look like if we used Shabbat, a day of rest and return to a more spiritual existence, to listen and take notice of the microaggressions in sacred spaces of worship, the Shabbat table, and communal gatherings? How can we model a healing masculinity and recognize how we take up space; from manspreading to mansplaining? How can we seek and offer enthusiastic, affirmative consent, even in platonic spaces?

When we didn't listen to the brokenness of the world, the destruction and shouting only amplified. Once again the cries of unholy inequality plague our society. Just as at Sinai, despite our fears, it is our obligation to hear the voices and fulfill the promise of not just learning, but also doing.[144]

---

[144] Exodus 24:7 נַעֲשֶׂה וְנִשְׁמָע.

Knowledge Equality[145]

Love is powerful. It can also be hard to predict. The *midrash*[146] tells the story of a wealthy woman who is curious about what God is doing now that the world has been created:

מַטְרוֹנָה שָׁאֲלָה אֶת רַבִּי יוֹסֵי בַּר חֲלַפְתָּא אָמְרָה לוֹ לְכַמָּה יָמִים בָּרָא הַקָּדוֹשׁ בָּרוּךְ הוּא אֶת עוֹלָמוֹ, אָמַר לָהּ לְשֵׁשֶׁת יָמִים, כִּדְכְתִיב (שמות כ, יא): כִּי שֵׁשֶׁת יָמִים עָשָׂה ה' אֶת הַשָּׁמַיִם וְאֶת הָאָרֶץ. אָמְרָה לוֹ מַה הוּא עוֹשֶׂה מֵאוֹתָהּ שָׁעָה וְעַד עַכְשָׁו, אָמַר לָהּ, הַקָּדוֹשׁ בָּרוּךְ הוּא יוֹשֵׁב וּמְזַוֵּג זִוּוּגִים...קָשָׁה הִיא לִפְנֵי הַקָּדוֹשׁ בָּרוּךְ הוּא כִּקְרִיעַת יַם סוּף

A noble woman asked Rabbi Yossi bar Chalafta a theological question: "How many days did it take the Holy One, blessed be God, to create the world?" He answers with the obvious

---

145 Originally offered as a speech under the chuppah of two amazing women.
146 Bereishit Rabbah 68:4.

"Six days" and offers the proof text from Exodus 20:11 "For in six days Hashem made the Heavens and the Earth". She follows up with "So what then is God doing [once the world is already created] until now?" The Rabbi responds, "God is sitting and making matches…and it is as difficult, before God, as the splitting of the sea."

It is interesting that Rabbi Yossi bar Chalafta compares Divine matchmaking to the miracle of the splitting of the sea. The Jerusalem Talmud[147] explains that when the Israelites came to the sea, with the Egyptians closing in on them, they were divided into four different opinions of what to do next. Some wanted to fight, while others preferred returning to Egypt. There was a group that desired to scream out and another segment thought to drown themselves in the sea. However, no one was able to imagine the sea splitting. Perhaps in that way, anticipating who can create a loving partnership with another is as difficult as the splitting of the sea.

Now, like then, creating a path forward relies on an expansiveness of possibilities—one which, until it happens, feels impossible and unimaginable. But once it happens, it will forever be celebrated and cherished.

As we prepare today for the giving of the Torah, and we re-experience our collective wedding, we remind ourselves that love and unity with each other is what enabled us to merit the Divine Revelation at Mount Sinai, where we stood "like one person with one heart".

---

[147] Taanit 2:5.

The Rabbis[148] note that when Jacob gathered his children together on his deathbed, the loving wholeness of the family allowed them access to a concealed truth that was the natural consequence of unlocking collective wisdom.

וַיִּקְרָא יַעֲקֹב אֶל־בָּנָיו וַיֹּאמֶר הֵאָסְפוּ וְאַגִּידָה לָכֶם אֵת אֲשֶׁר־יִקְרָא אֶתְכֶם בְּאַחֲרִית הַיָּמִים:

And Jacob called his sons and said, "Gather together that I may tell you what is to befall you in days to come."[149]

The closer we come to each other, the more we can understand the Divine in another. A congregation, in Hebrew a קהל—*Kahal*, alludes to this in that it is a community's shared experiences that grant access to wisdom.[150]

The Gemara tells us that before our *neshama* is allowed to come into this world it must take an oath; to be righteous and not to be wicked. As Yom Kippur begins, we remember all of our oaths and vows, including this first commitment at birth. It is perhaps for that reason that *Kol Nidrei,* while not halachically binding, is such a powerful liturgical component of Yom Kippur. It helps us focus and maintain a clarity of our responsibilities in relationship with God.

The vows that are going to be offered here are no different. The two brides have articulated their commitments to each other and

---

[148] Sees Tzror HaMor on verse.
[149] Genesis 49:1.
[150] Similar to Kohelet—Ecclesiastes, as a collection of knowledge.

the aspirations of their relationship. We, as a community, bear witness and support this public declaration of holiness and in doing so gain a greater understanding of the power of love.

Some things are too magnificent to be contained in a technical category. The Rema, in the Code of Jewish Law,[151] writes concerning Kol Nidrei:

והא דאמרינן כל נדרי בליל יום כיפורים הוי כאילו התנו בהדיא ומכל מקום לא סמכינן על זה להתיר בלא שאלה לחכם כי אם לצורך גדול

As for us, when we say Kol Nidrei on the eve of Yom Kippur, it is as if we are making this condition. Nonetheless, we do not rely on this to permit things without asking the rabbis, except for urgent cases.

It is impossible to say that this universally anticipated and celebrated, climatic liturgical introduction to the holiest day of the High Holidays just doesn't work. But rather it is achieving something else. It occupies a different space of holiness.

The Kol Nidrei ceremony[152] begins with the leaders of the community taking out the Torahs from the ark and reciting אוֹר זָרֻעַ לַצַּדִּיק וּלְיִשְׁרֵי לֵב שִׂמְחָה, "Light is sown for the righteous and for the aligned heart there is joy."[153] The essence of righteousness is pursuing goodness with all of one's strength. It is the quest to

---

[151] Yoreh De'ah 211:1.
[152] Getting married is compared to the day of Yom Kippur in terms of forgiveness of sins.
[153] Psalms 97:3.

achieve that goodness which invests in our future ability to finally experience that light.

We recognize, with gratitude, all of those whose sacrifices made this possible. And we rejoice, with the widest of hearts, that the future promise of "it does get better", is now.

Mazel Tov.

Tamuz

Transphobia is Not a Jewish Value[154]

Reb Yisroel Salanter, the founder of the modern *mussar* movement, taught "Not everything one thinks, should be said. Not everything that one says, should be written. And not everything one writes, should be published." I'm writing this article because the recent transphobic piece published in *Tablet Magazine*, never should have been written.

Thinking that support for trans and gender fluid people is motivated by financial profit is the type of offensive and harmfully ridiculous thought that belongs with others like: the Earth is flat, or

---

[154] Originally published for Bayit on June 20, 2022.

that Trump is still president. It does not belong in a publication that rational people are meant to take seriously.

Healthy exchanges of varied perspectives are essential for exploring the world of ideas and developing a better understanding of complex concepts. Now more than ever, we need to come together, respectfully, in conversation about things that reasonable people can disagree about. However, there is nothing respectable or reasonable about transphobia.

Questions affecting the practices of gender-queer Jews are real, complicated, and usually person specific. As in every other area of Jewish Law there are different opinions, perspectives, and a lot more to learn. Denying the reality of the lived experiences of people doesn't advance any thought or expand any understanding. It peddles a world of make-believe where all of the non-cis folks have been erased, and that world is most definitely flat.

Mishnah Avot[155] teaches that "כָּל מַחֲלֹקֶת שֶׁהִיא לְשֵׁם שָׁמַיִם, סוֹפָהּ לְהִתְקַיֵּם—Every dispute that is for the sake of Heaven, will in the end endure". The dispute of Korach, קרח, is offered by the Mishnah as the paradigmatic example of one that is not for the sake of Heaven. Instead of being discerning and engaging in an exacting pursuit of being חקר, he refused to take part in an honest analysis.

Every *chakira* has two sides: alternative ways of perceiving something. Rashi describes Korach as being a פקח, meaning clever, but instead of advocating for the advantages of one over the other, the Zohar claims that Korach was arguing against שלום—the wholesomeness of peace. He took himself to one צד "side",

---

[155] 5:17.

abandoning the collective. The word "שלום" has a numerical value of 376, twice as much as "פקח",[156] that relies on an appreciation of both "sides", צד, each having a value of 94.

One of the many lessons members of the cis community can learn from our gender queer siblings is how to better simplify the complexities of coexisting identities. This is reflected in the phrase mentioned above, לְשֵׁם שָׁמַיִם—in the name of Heaven. Tradition teaches that God blended "fire", אש, with "water", מים, to literally form the name of "Heaven"—לְשֵׁם שָׁמַיִם .

There are many things that are hidden and concealed from our limited grasp of the universe. Knowing what we don't know is an important prerequisite for acquiring wisdom, and also plays a role in our faith, going past what we can see. As we discover new truths and gain additional insights we shouldn't feel disoriented, but curious to learn more.

When Korach went out to protest, he wore a garment made entirely of תכלת—*techelis* (sky blue wool), asking if it required *tzitzit* (fringes). Our rabbis explain that Korach's superficial confidence in his own lack of awareness contributed to his heresy and resulted in his being swallowed by the ground. The rabbis understood that the heavens aren't actually blue, but that is simply how it appears to us when we look up at the sky. The *techelis* gets its name because its purpose—תכלית is to hold the space of perspective: to see and remember there is something beyond.

The Talmud teaches that when the rabbis were about to enter into the mystical orchard, Rebbe Akiva warned them that when they

---

[156] Which is 188.

reach the pure marble—שׁישׁ, they shouldn't say "water, water" even though the stones will appear that way. Accessing deeper realities requires a belief in experiences not limited to one's own. "שׁישׁ" is meant to be parsed שׁי-שׁ—that there is. Uncovering the Divine truth necessitates a faith in what hasn't yet been revealed.

Feeling threatened by those who are perceived as different and responding to the unknown through hate, fear, and denial is a synthetic response to the very human reaction of knowing that we don't know it all. Transgender, gender non-conforming, non-binary, fluid, and all the unique blends of gender identity are beautiful, holy, and part of God's plan. This is a simple truth, and it shouldn't have to be written.

Building Not Burying[157]

Can individuals be trusted to safely own lethal weapons or should a society restrict access to weapons in the name of public safety? The debate about gun control in America often becomes a discussion of balancing personal rights and public harm. Jewish tradition, which explores at length the relationship between individual and communal responsibilities, has much to contribute to this discussion.

The Mishnah[158] famously declares "אָדָם מוּעָד לְעוֹלָם", which is understood to mean that people are always held responsible for themselves and for actions that their bodies do. Yet, despite this focus on individual agency, the Torah also commands us:[159] "כִּי

---

[157] Originally published in "All Who Can Protest" July 2022 and co-authored with Rabba Wendy Amsellem.
[158] Bava Kama 2:6.
[159] Deuteronomy 22:8.

תִּבְנֶה בַּיִת חָדָשׁ וְעָשִׂיתָ מַעֲקֶה לְגַגֶּךָ—When you build a new house, you shall make a fence around your roof."

Even though the Torah expects each of us to be careful, when there is a known danger, we are obligated to mitigate it. Those who oppose gun control legislation often argue that laws are not needed; people should just be more careful. The Torah argues that in the face of a threat to life, we must be anticipatorily cautious. Furthermore, the Torah warns:[160] "וְלֹא־תָשִׂים דָּמִים בְּבֵיתֶךָ כִּי־יִפֹּל הַנֹּפֵל מִמֶּנּוּ—so that you will not incur bloodguilt, if a person were to fall from it."

Failure to build a fence around the roof makes the owner of the roof guilty of bloodshed if someone dies by falling off. If we do not act decisively to stem the free flow of guns in our society, we too will be guilty of דָּמִים בְּבֵיתֶךָ, "blood guilt" on ourselves.

The verse immediately preceding the commandment of fencing the roof seems unrelated and motivated by a strange intention. We are told: "שַׁלֵּחַ תְּשַׁלַּח אֶת־הָאֵם וְאֶת־הַבָּנִים תִּקַּח־לָךְ לְמַעַן יִיטַב לָךְ וְהַאֲרַכְתָּ יָמִים—Let the mother [bird] go, and take only the young, in order that you may fare well and have a long life."

The medieval exegete Rashi explains that if we send away the mother bird, we will merit new homes and be able to also fulfill the commandment of building fences on our roofs, as one good deed pulls along the next. It also frames the motivation as preparation for better human interactions.

---

[160] Ibid.

When we develop sensitivities to beings, we see new opportunities to build better structures and learn lessons in easy, preventative ways. Sending away the mother bird so that she does not suffer as she sees her young taken, encourages us to be alert to the needs of all of God's creatures. This stance of watchful, premeditated concern is praised by King Solomon in the Proverbs:[161] " צוֹפִיָּה (הילכת) [הֲלִיכוֹת] בֵּיתָהּ וְלֶחֶם עַצְלוּת לֹא תֹאכֵל—She anticipates the ways of her household, and does not eat the bread of laziness."

We must be proactive in expecting incipient dangers and act with alacrity to prevent tragedy.

Halachah also reflects this principle in a procedural distinction from affixing a mezuzah. The Sifri quotes Rebbe, "משעת חדושו עשה לו מעקה" which is understood by the Netziv to mean even before the house is finished we are invited to take the necessary actions to protect the wellbeing of others. Unlike the mezuzah, which is invalid if placed on the doorpost before the house is complete, this physical barrier to harm can't come early enough.

In the natural order of the world, children are meant to outlive their parents. The promise of a "good and long life", for treating animals with care, is meant to be extended to the broader human experience when we can start prioritizing the safety of people over the perceived needs of weapons. Children are referred to by the Talmud as "builders"; we should be supporting them, not the complacent evil that is causing them to be buried before their parents.

Taking Pride in the Parade[162]

Today is the Pride March, marking 50 years from Stonewall and the beginning of the modern chapter of the LGBTQ liberation movement. So much has been achieved and still so much is left to do.

As rabbis and allies we want to build and tend spaces that provide complete inclusion and equality. The daily reminders of the brokenness of this world help guide the work we do. The fight for LGBTQ rights is only necessary because society is defective. If there was no homophobia we wouldn't need straight allies. We only need a trans day of remembrance because many have forgotten that trans folks are God's folks. Our activism is necessitated by our communal failures.

---

[162] Originally published for Bayit on June 30, 2019 and co-authored with Rabba Wendy Amsellem.

Protests to dismantle socially constructed divisions and calls for radical inclusivity are nothing new. Korach and 250 of his followers bring these demands to Moses in a dramatic confrontation.

Korach and his entourage say to Moses and Aaron,[163] "It is too much, all of the nation is holy and God dwells within us all—why are you imposing a hierarchy on us?" At first glance, Korach's argument seems to be a model of inclusion. All of us are spiritually elevated and divinely inspired. Indeed, Korach is echoing a promise that God held out to Israel at Sinai,[164] "And you will be a kingdom of priests and a holy nation." Given Korach's supernal desires, why do he and his followers end up swallowed by a hole in the ground? The rabbinic tradition places Korach in a unique position: apparently punishing him for being ahead of his time. In Psalm 92, the song of Shabbat, we say "צַדִּיק כַּתָּמָר יִפְרָח כְּאֶרֶז בַּלְּבָנוֹן יִשְׂגֶּה—A righteous person will flourish like a date palm, and like a cedar, will grow tall". The last letters of the first three words of the verse in Hebrew spell Korach's name and there is a tradition that this foretells that Korach will flourish eventually as a righteous person.

The mystics[165] understand Korach to have been motivated by the yearning to get back to the place before the brokenness by asserting that we had already fixed it. However, if we do not acknowledge what is broken, we will not be able to properly rebuild. God's justice is necessary and restorative because divine punishments are consequences of our inappropriate actions and position us to repent and return to that ideal place. Korach's aspirations are holy,

---

[163] Numbers 16:3.
[164] Exodus 19:6.
[165] Zohar and Ari z"l.

it's his lack of awareness of the effort still needed to replace what was removed that is offensive to God's experience with humanity.

While Korach may have wanted to get back to the moment that God offered to make Israel an entirely holy nation of priests, he is in fact ignoring many of the events of the previous year. Since Israel encountered God at Sinai, they sinned by building and worshiping a Golden Calf and were almost destroyed. The firstborn sons no longer have a cultic role; they have been replaced by the Levites. Aaron's two sons died because they brought an unauthorized fire in the Tabernacle. And most recently, in last week's *parsha*, the nation has sinned by believing the slanderous report of the spies. As a result, God has condemned Israel to wander in the wilderness for the next forty years. Korach and his followers aspire to return to the spiritual state that Israel was in at Sinai. A year later though, the people are different. Pretending that nothing has shifted does not help them get closer to where they were.

As we celebrate the monumental strides that our country has made in removing LGBTQ discrimination, we must take care not to be like Korach and assert precipitously that all has been fixed. Walking around a city adorned with rainbow flags and stores capitalizing on Pride merchandise can be a beautiful and healing experience. But it also can make it harder to remember that we still have a day on the calendar, every year, to remember victims of anti-trans violence. Until all of the human rights of the LGBTQ community have been restored, we must protest and resist the narrative that says we have made it and our work is done. We are indeed all holy and it is our task to see that Divine holiness is respected, in us all.

Av

Covenantal Restoration

The Book of Lamentations, which is read on Tisha B'Av, begins in the form of several consecutive alphabetical acrostics.[166] Rabbi Yochanan[167] explains that this is because the source of all of the brokenness of the world is in the rejection of the Torah's instructions, which were given through the Hebrew alphabet. This is perhaps the most fundamental teaching that Jewish tradition offers to the world: God is good and following in God's ways brings goodness to the world.

On the first night of Passover, which is always the same night of the week as Tisha B'Av, we are instructed to engage the child who

---

[166] See the Rokeach for ways that this is concealed in the first word "איכה".
[167] Sanhedrin 104a.

doesn't yet know how to ask with: אַתְּ פְּתַח לוֹ—you will begin [the conversation]. It is also interpreted[168] as a directive to start their teaching with the alphabet; *aleph* א through *tof* ת. These twenty-two letters of the Hebrew alphabet correspond to the twenty-two days from the 17th of *Tammuz,* when the first set of tablets were broken, until *Tisha B'Av* when the Temples were destroyed.

When we initiate a child's education with "אַתְּ פְּתַח לוֹ", we are also delivering an additional basic truth of the world: if you don't treat people well, then everyone will suffer. This simple teaching is contained in a more complex allusion through the word אַתְ, as an *AtBaSh* אתבש,[169] to demonstrate that even more advanced and complicated problems still contain this rudimentary formula. The Tur[170] provides the verse[171] על מצות ומרורים יאכלוהו—"they shall eat with unleavened bread and with bitter herbs" as the proof text to remind us of the connection between Passover and the 9th of Av.[172]

Although Tisha B'Av is the saddest day on the Hebrew calendar, we don't say *Tachanun,* a mournful set of prayers[173] on this day. We

---

[168] Tiferes Bunim.

[169] The At-Bash cipher is a particular type of monoalphabetic gematria formed by taking the alphabet and mapping it to its reverse, so that the first letter pairs with the last letter, א-ת, the second letter, ב, to the second-to-last letter, ש, and so on.

[170] Rabbi Jacob Ben Asher 1269–1340.

[171] Exodus 12:8.

[172] Here the *aleph* is the first night of Passover and the *tuf* is Tisha B'Av. The first 6 letters אבגדהו represent the 6 nights of Passover while the last 6 letters תשרקצפ corresponds to the 6 different holidays and the night of the week that they will fall out on the calendar. For example, this year the first night of Passover was Friday night, which means that the 9th of Av begins Friday night. See Simon 428 for an expanded explanation.

[173] Supplications which are omitted on the holidays and happy days.

believe that in the future it will be experienced as a festival.[174] The first night of Passover is the indicating sign to whether we, as a people, will finally be able to celebrate on Tisha B'Av. It provides the opportunity to achieve a level of unity, and communal responsibility for each other, that will end the bitterness of God's concealment, the consequence of our poor treatment of each other that was the cause of our enslavement in Egypt and the Temple's destruction.[175]

This theme informs the entire Haggadah and is meant to frame our experience on Tisha B'Av. From the ritual acts of dipping at the Seder, which are inspired by the brother's dipping of Joseph's coat into blood,[176] to the placement of an egg[177] on the seder plate.[178] We are meant to feel empowered to reclaim our national narrative and choose our own redemption. We even conclude the Seder with the song *Chad Gadya*, "the goat my father bought", retelling our story from the perspective of a reunited family.

The Exodus from Egypt is called "*Yetziat Mitzrayim*" while the Three Weeks are called "*Ben HaMitzrayim*".[179] Passover represents an inclusive gathering, as the verse says:[180] כָּל קְהַל עֲדַת־יִשְׂרָאֵל—all the assembled congregation of the Israelites. While the unleavened

---

[174] Zecharia 8:19 calls it a moed as does Lamentations 1:15. See Rambam in the end of the laws of tanis see also Tannis 29a.

[175] The language that is used is: סימן לקביעת המועדים—homileticly meaning that we will establish whether it is celebratory or not.

[176] See Ben Ish Chai.

[177] Shulchan Aruch 476:2 נראה לי הטעם משום שליל תשעה באב נקבע בליל פסח ועוד זכר לחורבן.

[178] The egg is the customary food served to a mourner and eaten on the eve of Tisha B'Av.

[179] Literally between the difficulties.

[180] Exodus 12:6.

bread is emblematic of the divisiveness of evil as it says:[181] חָמֵץ
חֶלְקָם—which can be parsed as "*chametz* divides".[182]

The Maggid section of the Haggadah begins: "This is the bread of affliction that our ancestors ate in Egypt". Our telling of the story is immediately, and awkwardly, disrupted with the recognition that "Anyone who is hungry come and eat." And then with a seemingly unrelated aspirational wish about the Temple: "This year we are here, next year we will be in Jerusalem."

This interruption is reminiscent, and perhaps sourced in Abraham's[183] pivoting to the needs of his guests,[184] while engaged in a conversation[185] with the Divine.[186] It also nods to the famous story of Kamtza and Bar Kamtza[187] centered around someone who was mistakenly invited to a dinner party, and then rejected when their correct identity is made known. The Talmud attributes the destruction of the Temple to the complacency of the privileged, having a place at the table, but not leveraging their power to make sure there is a place for the perceived other. These exclusionary practices contribute to a universal breakdown of human dignity and God responds by withholding our access to the holiest of spaces.

---

[181] Leviticus 6:10.

[182] מצה and קהל have the same numerical value just as חמץ and חלק.

[183] Abraham is called אברהם—as father of many nations—Genesis 17:5.

[184] *Hachnosas Orchim*, inviting guests, is an opportunity to model the correct way of being and gather people under the wings of the Divine. See Meir Einei Chachamim page 381.

[185] This verse is used as a proof text by Rebbe Yehudah in the name of Rav, Shabbat 127a, גְּדוֹלָה הַכְנָסַת אוֹרְחִין , מֵהַקְבָּלַת פְּנֵי שְׁכִינָה. Perhaps Passover is chosen as the festival to highlight this Mitzvah because Lot, on Passover, invited those same angels as guests and fed them Matzos. Genesis 19:3 and Rashi there.

[186] Genesis 18:3.

[187] Gitten 55.

The Torah calls the time of Passover *Chodesh HaAviv* אביב,[188] which is understood as coming from the language of father אב.[189] One interpretation is that this month is the source of all twelve months: אב-יב,[190] as it begins the calendar year for festivals. On a deeper level, it also means that it contains within it all of the potential goodness that will later be manifested in the world, particularly in the month of Av אב,[191] and a return to the proper order of the alphabet.

Sefer Yetzirah, an early mystical work, describes stones, *avanim*— אבנים, being used to build spiritual houses. The Gra, in his commentary on this work, explains that these stones are the letters, and the houses are words. Each one of us represents a letter[192] and just as the twelve stones under Jacob's head came together to become one,[193] we must also acknowledge the shared source of our souls[194] if we are going to build a world that is worthy to house the Divine Presence.

Teshuva, repentance, means a return to a proper way of being. It is also an invitation to return to the basics, to the Aleph Bet of Judaism. We must orient our efforts of reunification through deconstructing the systems that perpetuate these separations and restore the familiar love that we are expected to have for each other

---

[188] Exodus 23:15.
[189] Rashi.
[190] See Rabbanu B'chaya Exodus 13:4. יב are the Hebrew letters for twelve.
[191] See Mei HaShiloach *Parshat Ki Tisa*.
[192] The word for Israel—ישראל—is understood as an acronym for ריבוא יש ששים אותיות לתורה—there are 600,000 letters in the Torah. See Penei Yehoshua Kiddushin 30a.
[193] Genesis 28:11, Chullin 91b.
[194] Shar HaGilgulim introduction 17.

to create a healthy and happy home. אַתְּ פְּתַח לֹו—when the world is so broken that we don't even know how to ask, there is constructive comfort in our ability to build a better world from love.

Sanctifying Our Synagogues

In recent years I've come to appreciate, and even prefer, the traditional rabbinic salutation of *shalom aleichem*, "peace be upon you", over the colloquial and perfunctory "how are you doing"? Beyond the benefits of mindful intentionality, I find it increasingly difficult to answer the simple, even rhetorical question that isolates each of us from the bigger picture. When asked, I want to respond: "Well…I live in a world that is on fire and every day seems worse than the one before…Thanks for asking. How about you?" Something feels off in not naming the global reality that the world is really not doing ok, and if we are paying attention, we shouldn't be able to say that we are either.

Our rabbis[195] teach:

---

[195] Taanit 11a.

בִּזְמַן שֶׁהַצִּבּוּר שָׁרוּי בְּצַעַר, אַל יֹאמַר אָדָם: אֵלֵךְ לְבֵיתִי, וְאֹכַל וְאֶשְׁתֶּה, וְשָׁלוֹם עָלַיִךְ נַפְשִׁי

When folks are immersed in suffering, a person [who isn't suffering] may not say: I will go to my home and I will eat and drink, and peace be upon you, my soul.

Once we are aware of the troubles of the world, we are not permitted to retreat into our own spheres of perceived comfort. We have to acknowledge the pain of others and seek to alleviate it.

Rabbi Ahron Kotler, the Lakewood Rosh Yeshiva, offers two approaches to the consciousness of other people's suffering. When possible, a person should engage in a partnership of action and offer a solution to the problem, whether with financial resources or with strategic advice. However, not all difficult situations can be fixed with human intervention alone. Particularly when we feel like there is nothing that we can actively do, we are asked to feel the pain of the other and carry part of their burden in our hearts.

Synagogues, beyond the communal role that institutions should play in providing support to individuals, have a special responsibility to share in this struggle because of their power as a house of prayer. The Talmud[196] relates:

רַבָּה בַּר חִינָּנָא סָבָא מִשְּׁמֵיהּ דְּרַב: כֹּל שֶׁאֶפְשָׁר לוֹ לְבַקֵּשׁ רַחֲמִים עַל חֲבֵירוֹ וְאֵינוֹ מְבַקֵּשׁ—נִקְרָא חוֹטֵא

---

[196] Brachos 12b.

> Rabba bar Ḥinnana Sava said in the name of Rav: Anyone who can pray for mercy on behalf of another and does not ask, is called a sinner.

Praying without incorporating supplications for others contributes to an erasure of the lived experience of God, as well as those who are suffering. This is judged so harshly because God naturally aligns with those who are in pain, as King David[197] testifies: יִקְרָאֵ֥נִי וְאֶעֱנֵ֗הוּ עִמּֽוֹ־אָנֹכִ֥י בְצָרָ֑ה אֲחַלְּצֵ֗הוּ וַאֲכַבְּדֵֽהוּ—"One will call upon Me and I will answer them, I am with the one in distress—I will release them and honor them."

LGBTQ folks are among the most marginalized and disenfranchised within Jewish communities. They occupy that space with the concealed Divine, who we have forced back into the closet to hide as a result of our actions. It is essential to understand how the many forms of homophobia and transphobia have isolated, excluded, and traumatized so many of our siblings in order to restore our sanctuaries as a safe space for all, including God.

The trajectory in the verse in Psalms, from an amelioration of stress to an abundance of honor, models a path of restoration and healing. It is specifically in the places of historical dehumanization that a return to dignity must begin. Celebrating the presence of LGBTQ folks in our communities should take many forms, and an easy place to start is in reversing the long-established practice of not talking about them.

---

[197] Psalms 91:15.

Amplifying the voices of those that have been silenced or stigmatized can give soothing expression and access to the lived experiences of those who should never had been denied or ignored. Affirming and validating the many identities and orientations, from the mundane interactions of membership applications to the sacred relationships of rituals and gender based spiritual practice, should be elevated and appreciated.

When we listen to the painful realities of others, through their personal narratives, we are better informed when we make decisions in the future. It also reveals our unfortunate, and often unintended, past complicity in a dominant culture of harmful practices. Proximity to the lived stories of others not only brings us closer together, and to a more holistic understanding of the world, but it also empowers us to own our individual identities as holy agents of change, transforming our physical resources into spiritual ones. When we ally in solidarity with the afflicted, we bring the relief of God's presence and with it, the accompanying promise of a peaceful and more perfect existence for us all.

Allyship and Rebuilding the Temple[198]

In this month of Av, as we increased focus on the destruction of the Temple, we recall King David's description of Jerusalem, in all of its glory, as כְּעִיר שֶׁחֻבְּרָה־לָּהּ יַחְדָּו—a city that is tightly knit together.[199] The Jerusalem Talmud[200] understands this verse to mean that Jerusalem will be rebuilt only when it is a city where all are *chaverim*—bound in friendship. Our current status of *churban*—destruction, is the natural result of our lack of *chaburah*—connectedness. God's house can't be rebuilt until we lay the foundation with our mended relationships.

Constructing a physical structure today requires many specific skill sets and forms of expertise. Carpenters, electricians, plumbers and decorators all must work together to successfully support the

---

[198] Originally published for Bayit on August 2, 2022.
199 Psalms 122:3.
200 Chagigah 3:6.

collective project. If the needs of one are not understood or incorporated, then the finished product will be deficient.

Developing an inclusive and supportive community is no different. For this reason, the Talmud[201] instructs us to be in conversation with each other when learning Torah, ensuring that we understand the realities of each other. The proof text that is offered draws on the foolish arrogance of those who don't connect to the lived experience of others to inform their own understanding of the world:

כִּדְרַבִּי יוֹסֵי בְּרַבִּי חֲנִינָא, דְּאָמַר רַבִּי יוֹסֵי בְּרַבִּי חֲנִינָא: מַאי דִּכְתִיב "חֶרֶב אֶל הַבַּדִּים וְנֹאָלוּ"—חֶרֶב עַל שׂוֹנְאֵיהֶם שֶׁל תַּלְמִידֵי חֲכָמִים שֶׁיּוֹשְׁבִים בַּד בְּבַד וְעוֹסְקִים בַּתּוֹרָה

Rabbi Yosei, son of Rabbi Ḥanina, said: What is the meaning of that which is written: "A sword is upon the boasters, and they shall become fools"?[202] [This verse can be interpreted homiletically]: A sword upon the enemies of Torah scholars, a euphemism for the Torah scholars themselves, who sit alone and study Torah.

Those who learn Torah on their own are learning an incomplete Torah. They are lacking the perspectives, ideas, and access to the lived experiences of their fellow scholars.

---

[201] Brachos 63a.
[202] Jeremiah 50:36.

The opening verse of Lamentations[203] begins: אֵיכָה יָשְׁבָה בָדָד הָעִיר רַבָּתִי עָם—"Alas, she sits in solitude, the city that once contained multitudes of people". Solitude is both the cause of, and the attendant result of, a breakdown of community. The city of Jerusalem remains alone—בָדָד because of the self-centered behavior of her inhabitants—שֶׁיּוֹשְׁבִים בַּד בְּבַד.

The Rabbis teach: "Every generation in which the Temple is not rebuilt is faulted as if it had destroyed it".[204] Today, our continued failure to achieve complete acceptance, inclusivity, and celebration of LGBTQ Jews, often the most excluded and marginalized in many religious communities, calls on us all to be better allies. It is a path towards a communal restoration that could merit God's return to us, providing an unbroken home for all of God's children.

An ally, in Jewish tradition, is called a "*chaver*", literally one who is attached to another, like the Latin *alligare*—to bind together. A *chaver tov* is someone who is able to connect the good of the world to another.

Our current state of Temple destruction, exile, and Divine concealment is a consequence, not a punishment, of our divisiveness as a people. Making judgments based on fear and prejudice led the spies to bring a false report about the land of Israel. Mishnah Ta'anit[205] relates that the spies returned with their libel on Tisha B'Av. This incident, like transphobia and

---

[203] Which is read on the 9th of Av the day that the Temples were destroyed.
[204] Jerusalem Talmud Yoma 1:1.
[205] 4:6.

homophobia, has its source in the kind of blatant hatred that caused the second Temple to be destroyed.

The mystics observe that this physical breakdown of the ideal is simply a reflection of us disrupting the order of creation. They explain that in the Hebrew Alphabet, the letter ע which means "eye", precedes פ the "mouth" because we must first experience the proximity of something, gaining an informed perspective, in order to speak about it properly.

It is not coincidental that the letter immediately before ע is the ס which means "support" and is represented in the alphabetical acrostic of Ashrei[206] as "supports all who have fallen". Loving, particularly those who are suffering, doesn't require getting permission first.

The month of Av, a word which means "Father," reminds us both of the love that God still has for us in this estranged dynamic and also for our need to recognize the ways in which we have failed to provide and support each other as family. Learning how to engage and speak with people who are perceived as different, and overcome the dominant culture of divisiveness, is a necessary step in achieving a covenantal restoration, where we can return to an ideal relationship with God. If we can't come together in celebration of the Divine within people, then we will be destined to find ourselves mourning alone without the Temple.

---

[206] Psalms 145.

Protesting Conversion Therapy[207]

I was praying at the Kotel a couple of days ago when a Rosh Yeshiva, in Lakewood, New Jersey, reached out for advice. He has a student who is gay, and his parents want to send him for conversion therapy. This rabbi wanted to know what to tell the parents to convince them not to send him—he didn't want to traumatize the student that he cared for.

So I told him to explain to the parents that they have a choice. They can either have a gay son who is observant, or a gay son that is not observant. Or, God forbid, no son at all. Because when we force someone to choose between a religious identity and a queer/genderqueer identity, there is only one of them that is a choice.

_____

[207] Originally given as a speech at a protest in Tel Aviv in the summer of 2019.

The only thing that conversion therapy achieves is to convert people out of Judaism.

When the world wasn't such a safe place to come out people suffered in silence. But now, people have choices. We must end the horrific practice, and rabbinic malpractice, of forcing queer youth into heteronormative, mixed-orientation marriages.

Every day people come into my office after they find out that their partner is gay, and perhaps wasn't faithful. Often there is compassion for the spouse, until they learn that the rabbi who officiated knew that he was gay and still told him to marry her. The anger and resentment is justifiable.

What people do, or don't do, is between them and God. We, however, need to own this climate of homophobia. Not just that we are complicit in it, but that we have created it.

Allyship is awkward because it is predicated on the world being broken. But that brokenness invites and obligates us to step up and fix it.

We must elevate the most pronounced identity of every human being: Ethiopian, Palestinian, immigrant, even *charedi*,[208] to that of being created in the image of the Almighty.

To the LGBTQ youth, especially the trans and gender non-conforming, we see you. We love you. God doesn't put extra people in this world; we need you.

---

[208] Israeli term for Ultra Orthodox.

Seasonal Resistance

It does get better.

Elul

Building Communal Resistance[209]

Resist so that you may exist. This is the charge that the Torah[210] provides as an introduction to communal living in the Land of Israel. The statutes that follow demand that we end our apathy towards injustice. We must mobilize a resistance in which those with societal privilege feel as freighted by maltreatment in the world as those who suffer indignity directly.

God's design for building a holier world has an interesting and perhaps counter-intuitive prerequisite. According to R' Yossi HaGalili, the Torah lists categories of military deferment—those who built a new house, planted a vineyard or got betrothed, who might be distracted because they haven't yet finished those

---

[209] Originally published for Bayit on September 1, 2019.
[210] Deuteronomy 16:20.

pursuits—only to provide cover for the one true military exemption: one who is fearful and faint hearted.[211] The Talmud re-contextualizes this fear as someone afraid of their transgressions—המתיירא מעבירות שבידו.[212]

Being concerned about one's sins is not a bad thing: not being afraid of them is a much greater cause of concern. Why, then, should tradition disqualify someone from participating in this resistance on account of a level of spiritual consciousness?

The Torah's word for fear here "הירא" is found in only one other verse in the Torah. After Moses declares that the plague of hail is coming, the verse states: "Whoever among the servants of Pharaoh feared the word of Hashem chased his servants and his livestock into the houses".[213] This inward-focused fear is limited to retribution for sin, a concern for the safety of oneself and one's possessions. This preoccupation of "שבידו"—that which specifically affects "oneself"—disqualifies a person from participating in communal action.

The point is that motive matters. It's one thing to oppose nearly daily mass shootings by white domestic terrorists because you are afraid to get shot. It's another to act because no one should get shot! No movement fully can succeed if each participant's motive is mainly one's own needs, spiritually or physically.

Our relationship with God also must transcend limited self-interest. Today is Rosh Chodesh Elul (אלול), intensifying our personal

---

introspection into our intimate and unique relationship with God. Elul's name is famously understood as an acronym for the Hebrew verse in Song of Songs, "I am to my beloved and my beloved is to me—אֲנִי לְדוֹדִי וְדוֹדִי לִי".[214] What is less known is that it also refers to the sin of Judah's son Onan, who marries Tamar after his older brother Er dies.[215] Judah instructs Onan to marry Tamar in order to establish a line of descent for his deceased brother. The verse explains that Onan knew that the child of this levirate marriage wouldn't be considered his ("לֹא לוֹ"), and therefore refused to have a child with her.

Tradition responded to Onan's fit of pique by leaving him out of our spiritual future. Our rabbis teach that the Messiah will come from the union of Judah and Tamar, along with Ruth and Boaz. Both Levirate marriages, that would produce children credited to others. Redemption comes from exactly this quality of selflessness.

That's why a spiritually authentic אלול must also include the לֹא לוֹ. Elul focuses us on precisely what is beyond ourselves. True *teshuvah* requires restoration for all. We must love, protect, and provide for asylum seekers, trans youth, and all suffering prejudice, discrimination, or other indignities. Redemption and forgiveness only can come when we restore our love for each other the way we naturally love ourselves.

---

[214] Song of Songs 6:3.
[215] Genesis 38:9.

Repentance for Earthlings[216]

The story is told about two people who are disputing ownership over a piece of land, each claiming that it belongs to them. A rabbi is consulted to offer a ruling in Jewish Law to decide the case. After carefully listening to the arguments of both sides he says "Ok, now I need to hear what the land has to say about it". With quite a bit of hesitation, both parties finally agree to accompany the Rabbi to the parcel of land in question. The Rabbi kneels down, gently placing his ear to the ground. After a few moments, the Rabbi stands up and relates to the two concerned litigants: "The land says that you are both wrong. In the end you each will belong to it."

We are in relationship with the Earth, and the Torah expects us to ensure that it is a healthy one. King Solomon reminds us[217] "All go to the same place; all originate from dust and all return to dust".

---

[216] Originally published for Earth Etude on September 5, 2022.
[217] Ecclesiastes 3:20.

However, each of us must take ownership over our actions, and inactions, for the time in between.

Adam, the original person whose name means "Earthling" and now includes all of humanity, is told "It is not good to be alone" and therefore God "made a helper against them".[218] The commentaries explain that this partnership is necessary lest a person make a mistake to think that they are completely self-sufficient and can live independent of the world around them.

It is perhaps for this reason that the phrase "*ki tov*—it was good", which is used to describe all other creations, is missing from Adam's formation. Humans alone cannot be good—we must always honor the dynamic with our environment. This principle is reinforced with the odd language at the end of the verse "a helper against them". It is understood that if we respect our role in relationships, then they can be supportive and helpful to us in becoming the best versions of ourselves. If, however, we are not acting appropriately, then the natural consequence will be an opposition.

Our Rabbis understand that this pushback is also beneficial feedback that is a healthy part of the goodness of coexistence. Constructive responses provide an opportunity to re-adjust and make informed course corrections, but only if we are ready to receive them.

God spoke this world into existence through soft and gentle speech. Because of the harm we have caused it, the earth is now screaming out in rageful protest. If we continue to act as if we

---

[218] Genesis 2:18.

control the Earth, we will soon be reminded that it actually owns us.

Selichot and Self Doubt[219]

The opening psalm of *Kabbalat Shabbat*[220] begins in celebration[221] "לְכוּ נְרַנְּנָה—*Lechu Neranena*—Let us sing joyfully" but concludes with a critical judgment of the Jewish People. After forty years in the desert, the Israelites are described as errant hearted, and not knowing God's way:

אַרְבָּעִים שָׁנָה אָקוּט בְּדוֹר. וָאֹמַר עַם תֹּעֵי לֵבָב הֵם. וְהֵם לֹא יָדְעוּ דְרָכָי.[222]

It's hard to understand how we, today, can be expected to get it right, when the generation that saw and experienced it all still wasn't able to figure it out.

---

[219] Originally offered as a *drusha* in Austin, Texas before Selichot.
[220] Psalms 95:1.
[221] One of the 11 chapters authored by Moses.
[222] Psalms 95:10.

This might be one of the lessons of repentance, to revisit something in the past, with a different perspective that only time can assist in providing. Who we are this year is hopefully more evolved than last year's version. Forty years is a long time to reflect.[223] However, according to this week's Torah portion, it seems like they finally succeeded.

וְלֹא־נָתַן֩ ה' לָכֶ֨ם לֵב֙ לָדַ֔עַת וְעֵינַ֥יִם לִרְא֖וֹת וְאָזְנַ֣יִם לִשְׁמֹ֑עַ עַ֖ד הַיּ֥וֹם הַזֶּֽה:

Yet, until this day Hashem has not given you a heart to understand, or eyes to see, or ears to hear.[224]

This verse is not describing literal seeing and hearing but rather emphasizing the need to expand our perception beyond the limited physical plane of presentation. The first letter of each of the three words—לָדַ֔עַת לִרְא֖וֹת לִשְׁמֹ֑עַ forms דרש—*drash*, to expound.[225] A *drashah*, the colloquial word for sermon, has its source in "וְדָרַשְׁתָּ֧ וְחָקַרְתָּ֛ וְשָׁאַלְתָּ֖ הֵיטֵ֑ב—you shall investigate and inquire and interrogate thoroughly".[226] Although, and perhaps because, the Israelites witnessed the miraculous, there was something deficient in the depth of their comprehension until this day where God offers rebuke and empowers them with the clarity of choice.[227]

---

[223] The Talmud, Avodah Zarah 5b teaches that it takes forty years for a student to understand the words of their teacher. אמר רבה ש"מ לא קai איניש אדעתיה דרביה עד ארבעין שנין.

[224] Deuteronomy 29:3.

[225] See Lechem Shlomo page 706.

[226] Deuteronmy 13:15.

[227] See Kovetz Sichos for additional approaches.

So what was so special about this day? The Rabbis teach that this was the day that Moses died.[228] One of the ongoing struggles that the Jewish People faced in the desert was their ability to relate directly to God, without an intermediary. The sin of the golden calf begins with the declaration[229]

עֲשֵׂה־לָנוּ אֱלֹהִים אֲשֶׁר יֵלְכוּ לְפָנֵינוּ כִּי־זֶה מֹשֶׁה הָאִישׁ אֲשֶׁר הֶעֱלָנוּ מֵאֶרֶץ מִצְרַיִם לֹא יָדַעְנוּ מֶה־הָיָה לוֹ:—

When the people saw that Moses was so long in coming down from the mountain, the people gathered against Aaron and said to him, "Come, make us a god who shall go before us, for that fellow Moses—the man who brought us from the land of Egypt—we do not know what has happened to him."

Rashi understands that a "heart to know" was necessary on this day: לְהַכִּיר אֶת חַסְדֵי הַקָּבָּ"ה וְלִדַּבֵּק בּוֹ—"to recognize the kindness of Hashem and to cleave to it". It is perhaps for this reason that *Selichot* tonight begins with a recognition that God is the source of righteousness: "לְךָ ה הַצְּדָקָה".[230]

We just read in the *Haftorah*, in preparation, from the prophet Isaiah "וְעַמֵּךְ כֻּלָּם צַדִּיקִים—your people are all righteous",[231] because we need the reminder. Particularly when we come to ask forgiveness

---

[228] See Meshech Chochmah here.
[229] Exodus 32:1.
[230] Daniel 9:7.
[231] Isaiah 60:21.

and reflect on all of our mistakes and shortcomings, it's important to not lose a sense of our own worth and holiness.

Ki Tavo is the fiftieth *parsha* in the Torah. The letter *nun*—נ has the numerical value of fifty and represents falling (*nefelia*) it also makes up the left side of the letter *tzadik*—צ representing the physical desire of the body to lean towards its source, the ground. The letter *yud*—י remains and alludes to the *yid*; the spiritual side of us that seeks elevation.[232]

These two aspects of ourselves can create tension and doubt, confusing us as to who we really are. This is true on a personal and national level.

The Zohar[233] teaches that there are fifty reminders of the exodus from Egypt in the Torah[234] and the fiftieth is in this week's portion, as part of the speech of bringing the first fruits.[235] An essential aspect of coming into the land with confidence and faith is going out from the mindset of enslavement. To help us achieve a greater sense of freedom, on the night of Passover, we include this section in the Haggadah highlighting our spiritual identity.

Moving beyond a state of "moving beyond" takes work.[236] Diving deeply into the goodness of God draws us closer to that Goodness. Elul provides the proximity for us to more easily perceive the

---

[232] See Sefer HaChaim.
[233] 2:85b.
[234] See the Gra on *tikkunim* 32.
[235] Megaleh Amukos.
[236] A going out of going out—יציאה from a mentality of יציאה.

perfect nature of God, that we are often distracted from the rest of the year.

The true discomfort in repentance isn't about returning to a place that is better for us, but in the awkwardness in owning that we chose to be away from it. Denying our claim to be part of that goodness can only be made when we don't understand our inseparable relationship to God. The more we expand our capacity to experience God's goodness, the closer we are to knowing that we are home.

The Blessing of Community[237]

The mystical tradition understands the Hebrew alphabet as the building blocks of creation. The Kabbalists parse the verse: "בְּרֵאשִׁית בָּרָא אֱלֹהִים אֵת..." In the beginning God created "et"—the **aleph** through the **tav**. These letters, and subsequently this world, originate with the Torah itself. Rashi explains the first word "בְּ-רֵאשִׁית": with the Torah, which is called "*reshiet*", God created the world.

The Zohar describes how each letter of the alphabet argued with God that it should get to be the first letter in the Torah. Aleph proposes that it should start the Torah as it is the first letter in the alphabet. "That is true," God responds, "but the word "ארור" meaning "curse" also begins with an *aleph* and it wouldn't be fitting to start the Torah with curses." Instead it would be most

---

237 Originally offered as a *drasha* in Wellington, New Zealand.

appropriate to open with the *bet*, which represents *brachah*, blessing. However, God consoles the aleph by placing it at the beginning of the Ten Commandments with the word *Anochi*—אנכי—"I".

The Bal Haturim teaches that this "*Anochi*" makes an appearance in the introduction to this week's Torah portion: רְאֵה אָנֹכִי נֹתֵן לִפְנֵיכֶם הַיּוֹם בְּרָכָה וּקְלָלָה—See this day I set before you blessing and curse".[238] A simple interpretation is that just as we have a choice to follow the Ten Commandments and be rewarded by God, we also have a choice to fulfill all of God's *mitzvot* and to then merit God's blessings.

In addition, both the Ten Commandments and the opening verse of *Parshat Re'eh* describe an act of seeing. In Exodus[239] we are told...וְכָל־הָעָם רֹאִים אֶת־הַקּוֹלֹת —"and the whole nation saw the sounds" and here in Deuteronomy the people are asked to "look" at the stark moral choice they must make.

Perhaps on a deeper level—and supported by the shift from the singular "see" to the plural "in front of"—רְאֵה אָנֹכִי נֹתֵן לִפְנֵיכֶם—the verse is an allusion to the singular unity of the Jewish people at the giving of the Ten Commandments as it says: כְּאִישׁ אֶחָד בְּלֵב אֶחָד—like one person with one heart.[240] With this understanding, Moses is revealing that the source of blessing is in our togetherness.

Each one of us has a choice of where we place ourselves in relation to community. Bringing attention to this daily opportunity רְאֵה אָנֹכִי נֹתֵן לִפְנֵיכֶם הַיּוֹם בְּרָכָה וּקְלָלָה—see [your] "**I**" is given before you

---

[238] Deuteronomy 11:26.
[239] 20:15.
[240] See Rashi there.

today, as a blessing or a curse—encourages us to ask, "How do we choose to be ourselves in healthy, holy, and impactful ways?" Where is our "I", *ani*?

Hillel famously taught "אִם אֵין אֲנִי לִי, מִי לִי"—If I am not for myself, **who** will be for me?", because no one else is me, who is capable of making my unique contributions. The other extreme is seemingly even more dehumanizing: "וּכְשֶׁאֲנִי לְעַצְמִי, מָה אֲנִי"—And if I am only for myself **what** am I?" One loses the quality of being a human by taking themselves out of humanity.

Parshat Re'eh is always read either on the Shabbat that we announce the month of Elul or, like today, at the beginning of the month. It is during this time, in preparation for Rosh Hashana, that we engage in deep introspection and focus on our behavior. It is essential for us to be reminded that every *ben adam l'chavaro*, interpersonal commitment, is a *ben adam l'makom*—a reflection on our dynamic with God. As we orient towards the Divine, as King Solomon wrote אֲנִי לְדוֹדִי וְדוֹדִי לִי—"I am to my beloved and my beloved is mine", we elevate the context of הָרֹעֶה בַּשּׁוֹשַׁנִּים; that we are part of a bigger flock. We can't show complete love to God without also showing love to each other. Where we direct our "I" informs God's response and reciprocation.

Talmud Bavli[241] teaches that Rosh Hashanah is celebrated on the anniversary of the sixth day of creation, the day on which humans were created and also the day of the first transgression. Adam and Eve's sin caused the letter *aleph* to be lost from several important roles in society. Part of our preparation for re-experiencing the Birthday of the World properly is in returning to the One, the *aleph*

---

[241] Rosh Hashanah see 16 and 27.

of the *Alufa Shel Olam*, Creator of the Universe, by recognizing and elevating God in each other. Blessings and curses are determined simply by our ability to connect to the source of goodness by seeing ourselves, singular, as part of the collective.

Tishri

Homophobia Hurts All of Us, Especially God[242]

Although the world was actually created five days earlier, on the twenty fifth of Elul, Rosh Hashanah is celebrated as the birthday of the world because God is אֱלֹהִים חַיִּים—desirous of life, and it was on the sixth day of creation that humanity came to be. However, life that doesn't honor its source is described as "better that they shouldn't have come into this world".[243]

The first special addition to the prayers on Rosh Hashanah, that is then included in every subsequent prayer through Yom Kippur, reinforces this point:

---

[242] Originally published for Keshet on September 28, 2022.
[243] Chagigah 11b.

זָכְרֵנוּ לְחַיִּים מֶלֶךְ חָפֵץ בַּחַיִּים וְכָתְבֵנוּ בְּסֵפֶר הַחַיִּים לְמַעַנְךָ אֱלֹהִים חַיִּים

Remember us for life King, Who desires life; and inscribe us in the Book of Life, for Your sake, Living God.

What is the intention that we are meant to have in describing God as a "Living God"? How does writing us in the Book of Life benefit God?

The Teferet Shlomo[244] frames being alive as having a positive impact in the world. He brings support from the Talmud's assertion that our patriarch Jacob never died.[245] Since his descendants continue to manifest the Divine Will in this world, it is as if Jacob is still living.[246] For this reason, when we begin the *parsha* in which Jacob leaves this world, the verse[247] says וַיְחִי יַעֲקֹב—and Jacob lived.[248]

This, he argues, is not limited to the human experience but also includes the Divine. God is given life, *kiviyachol*, when we honor God's intentions. The Teferet Shlomo parses the verse,[249] "אֲשֶׁר יַעֲשֶׂה אֹתָם הָאָדָם, וָחַי בָּהֶם אֲנִי יְקֹוָק", homiletically, as I, God, will live when you are being good people.

---

[244] Shlomo Hakohen Rabinowicz (1801–1866) was the first Rebbe of the Radomsk Hasidic dynasty.

[245] Tannis 5b.

[246] Teferes Shlomo on Rosh Hashanah.

[247] Genesis 47:28.

[248] Immediately after it says וַיִּפְרוּ וַיִּרְבּוּ מְאֹד at the end of 47:27. See Yodie Bina there.

[249] Leviticus 18:5.

Just as there is no king without a nation, God's existence as Creator of the World is given vitality through us honoring that identity. Because God is nourished by our good deeds, we pray that we are worthy to live a life that supports and satisfies God's desire to be in relationship with us.

It is particularly our interactions with God's creations that determine whether we are recorded in the Book of Life. Ben Azzai taught[250] " אֵיזֶהוּ מְכֻבָּד, הַמְכַבֵּד אֶת הַבְּרִיּוֹת, שֶׁנֶּאֱמַר כִּי מְכַבְּדַי אֲכַבֵּד וּבֹזַי יֵקַלּוּ[251]—Who is honored? One who honors their fellow human beings as it is said: 'For I honor those that honor Me, but those who spurn Me shall be dishonored".[252] When we dehumanize each other we are destroying Godliness.[253] Conversely, when we support the wellbeing and dignity of people we are giving life to God. The Hebrew words for "life—חיים" and for "a wise person—חכם" have the same numerical value[254] because "wisdom preserves the life of those who possess it".[255]

It is not coincidental that positions of homophobia and transphobia are irrational and indefensible. While refusing to acknowledge the existence of queer people in religious spaces is a convenient way of avoiding any thoughtful conversation, it does nothing to support their lived experiences, damages everyone involved, and denies the reality of truth.

---

[250] Pirkei Avos 4:1.

[251] Samuel 1:2.

[252] 1 Samuel 2:30.

[253] See Ruach Chaim.

[254] Degel Machaneh Ephraim in Deuteronomy.

[255] Ecclesiastes 7:12.

Where's the wisdom in guiding queer folks to marry people they are not attracted to? This erasure of human dignity powerfully obfuscates the otherwise obvious consequence that it is also forcing straight people to unknowingly marry someone who isn't attracted to them!

Who wins here? The institutions themselves are weakened by the absence of thought leadership. How can we trust in the wisdom of our tradition if those transmitting it are offering a world of make believe as a response to urgent questions of simply being.

Is being moved by the powerful blasts of the shofar spiritually significant if it doesn't contribute to one's sensitivity towards the actual cries of young students trying, unsuccessfully, to pray away their identity in isolation? Can one approach Rosh Hashanah, celebrating the birthday of the world, while excluding those who God created it for?

Prayer is described as the service of the heart.[256] If our hearts are closed off to the suffering that we have inflicted on so many of God's children, how open can God be to our prayers? Perhaps this is why the prefixes to each use of the words for "life"— זָכְרֵנוּ לְחַיִּים מֶלֶךְ חָפֵץ בַּחַיִּים וְכָתְבֵנוּ בְּסֵפֶר הַחַיִּים form the word לבה [257] "in one's heart"—are a prerequisite to connect to God as לְמַעַנְךָ אֱלֹהִים חַיִּים— "for God's sake".

---

[256] Taanis 2a.
[257] 1 Samuel 1:13 this is the word used for Chana's prayer.

Fulfilling Our Promise to Be

Much is offered, in the form of rabbinic advice, about the consequences of taking up too much space, excessive talking,[258] and even coveting what another has. As the Talmud[259] teaches:

שֶׁכָּל הַנּוֹתֵן עֵינָיו בְּמַה שֶׁאֵינוֹ שֶׁלּוֹ מַה שֶׁמְבַקֵשׁ אֵין נוֹתְנִין לוֹ וּמַה שֶׁבְּיָדוֹ נוֹטְלִין הֵימֶנּוּ

Whoever desires that which doesn't belong to them, what they want they won't be given to them, and what they already have, they will lose.

---

[258] Avos.

[259] Sotah 9a and see Students of Rosh in Drashas for more examples.

Less, however, is said about the severity of the transgression of misplaced silence, invisibility, or the lack of imagination. Over the last two days of Rosh Hashanah we were expected to reflect on who we are and what we are capable of achieving. Hopefully there were moments of inspiration, followed by internal commitments to actualize that potential. This process is not limited to any particular festival, however today, Tzom Gedaliah, highlights what happens when we have spiritual feelings and don't take action to manifest them.

2,444 years ago, after the first Temple was destroyed, Gedaliah ben Achikam was the governor of the remaining Jewish population. Shortly before Rosh Hashanah he was warned that someone who wanted the position for himself, was going to kill him for it. No precautions were taken and, as we remember every year on this day, Gedaliah and many others were murdered by a very small group of just eleven men. Because no one intervened to prevent this tragedy, the remaining Jewish population had to flee into exile.

There is a deeper connection between this particular day on the Hebrew calendar and the danger of leaving things unfulfilled. Our Rabbis teach that the Ten Days of Repentance correspond to the Ten Commandments.[260] Today, the third day of Tishri, aligns with "Don't take God's name in vain".[261] The B'er Moshe[262] writes that this also includes situations when we are inspired to do good, but don't follow through with it. Failing to bring that holiness in the world abandons and desecrates the wasted inspiration.

---

[260] See Sefat Emet Shabbat Shuvah 665.
[261] See Rosh Hashanah 18b that this is also the day the decree to include God's name on documents was annulled.
[262] *Parshat Yitro.*

We are meant to partner with the Divine, as co-creators, but it can be hard to ever be confident in knowing exactly how to fulfill our role. Hillel, who the Talmud[263] uses as the model for humility, famously taught:[264] אָם אֵין אֲנִי לִי, מִי לִי—"if I am not for myself who will be for me?". The mystical commentaries observe that the word for "nothing", אין, is the same letters for the word "I"—אני,[265] demonstrating that where we place ourselves makes all the difference.

Knowing what motivates us can guide us to where we should be. When Rav Shimon Schwab[266] was a young rabbinical student, he spent a Shabbat with the Chofetz Chaim[267]. The Chofetz Chaim was a Kohen, and asked Reb Shimon if he was one as well. When the young man responded in the negative, the Chofetz Chaim, who wanted to teach him an important lesson, followed up by asking "Why?". "Because my father wasn't a Kohen?" he answered cautiously.

The Chofetz Chaim lovingly explained: "There was once a time in Jewish history when our teacher Moses called out "מִי לַ'ה אֵלָי—**Who** is for God? Let them gather to me.'[268] My great-great grandfather answered the call and your great-great grandfather did not answer the call. That is why my father was a Kohen and your father was not a Kohen."

---

[263] Shabbat 30b.
[264] Avos 1:14.
[265] See Rema.
[266] (1908–1995).
[267] (1838–1933).
[268] Exodus 32:26.

This is the question that we are constantly meant to answer.

The first Psalm[269] that we read on the night of Rosh Hashanah asks:

מִי־יַעֲלֶה בְהַר־ה' וּמִי־יָקוּם בִּמְקוֹם קׇדְשׁוֹ

Who may ascend the mountain of the LORD?

Who may stand in His holy place?

These words were said while the *shulchan*, table, was brought into the Holy of Holies.[270]

King David answers in the following verse:

נְקִי כַפַּיִם וּבַר־לֵבָב אֲשֶׁר ׀ לֹא־נָשָׂא לַשָּׁוְא נַפְשִׁי וְלֹא נִשְׁבַּע לְמִרְמָה׃

One who has clean hands and a pure heart,
who has not taken a false oath by My life
or sworn deceitfully.

There are consequences to our communal failure to fulfill our vows and live up to the commitments we have in relationship with God. It is the silent majority that has to answer for the unholy changes in

---

[269] Psalms 24:3.

[270] See Teferet Bunim *Parshat Vayakhel*. לבב—heart—references learning as an act of repentance alluded to in the first and last letters of the Torah, being doubled.

society that are mobilized by the vocal minority. Being opposed to bad isn't the same as being an agent of good.

The very last Mishnah[271] is comprised of two teachings:

אָמַר רַבִּי יְהוֹשֻׁעַ בֶּן לֵוִי, עָתִיד הַקָּדוֹשׁ בָּרוּךְ הוּא לְהַנְחִיל לְכָל צַדִּיק וְצַדִּיק שְׁלֹשׁ מֵאוֹת וַעֲשָׂרָה עוֹלָמוֹת, שֶׁנֶּאֱמַר (משלי ח), לְהַנְחִיל אֹהֲבַי יֵשׁ וְאֹצְרֹתֵיהֶם אֲמַלֵּא. אָמַר רַבִּי שִׁמְעוֹן בֶּן חֲלַפְתָּא, לֹא מָצָא הַקָּדוֹשׁ בָּרוּךְ הוּא כְּלִי מַחֲזִיק בְּרָכָה לְיִשְׂרָאֵל אֶלָּא הַשָּׁלוֹם.

Rabbi Yehoshua ben Levi said: In the world to come the Holy One, Blessed be God, will make each righteous person inherit three hundred and ten worlds, for it is written: "That I may cause those that love me to inherit *yesh*—יֵשׁ (which has a numerical value of three hundred and ten); and that I may fill their treasuries." Rabbi Shimon ben Halafta said: the Holy One, Blessed be God, found no vessel that could contain blessing for Israel save that of peace.

Our place in the next world is determined by our choices to advance peace in this world. We must be the *yesh*—the someone, in order to acquire the *ein*—that which doesn't yet exist, by proactively creating peace as an alternative to the opposition.[272]

---

[271] Oktzin 3:12.
[272] See Bais Aharon.

Returning to Love Together

The word "Shabbat" means to return.[273] It is also one of God's names.[274] Shabbat Shuva then is a return to the return; reconnecting with the Source[275] in preparation for Yom Kippur, which is called שַׁבַּת שַׁבָּתוֹן—a Shabbat of Shabbaton.[276] We see this alluded to in the special Haftorah[277] which repeats שׁוּבָה יִשְׂרָאֵל—return Israel וְשׁוּבוּ—and return.

Tradition teaches that we are composed of two parts: the body and the soul. One is from the Earth and the other from Heaven.[278] These correspond to the two types of repentance: one out of fear

---

[273] See Divrei Emes on Leviticus and many others.

[274] בזוהר יתרו דף פ"ח ע"א

[275] As we sing in Lecha Dodi—כִּי הִיא מְקוֹר הַבְּרָכָה—She is the source of blessing.

[276] Leviticus 16:31.

[277] Hosea 14:2–3.

[278] The word for "soul" נשמה has the same numerical value as the heavens "השמים".

and the other from love.[279] Shabbat also has two categories: *shamor v'zachor*—guarding against the negative prohibitions, and performing the positive commandments.

Although both motivations for repentance contribute to better behavior, being driven by love is fundamentally different. One of the many significant consequences is that operating out of fear is physically exhausting and draining, leaving very little energy available to feel anything positive,[280] while investing in a relationship through love is nourishing and enhancing.[281]

On Shabbat we are given additional soul capacity[282] and as a result, Shabbat represents a return from, and to, love. "Shabbat Shalom"[283] is an acknowledgment of the necessity of unity to form completeness, both as an individual[284] and as a community.[285]

Each one of us has a unique aspect of good that doesn't exist in anyone else.[286] It is the nature of goodness to attract, and attach, to the goodness in others, while evil separates.[287] Just as loving

---

[279] See Sfat Emet 662 Shabbat Teshuva.

[280] See Chamra Tova parahas sh'menie.

[281] See Rav Dessler's essay on giving as the root of love.

[282] Beitzah 16a.

[283] "Shalom" means "peace", "complete", and is also a name of God.

[284] In the name of R' Tzvi Hirsch (brought in Bnei Yissaschar Shabbat) אהבה בכל לב. אהבה בכל נפש. אהבה—בגי' שבת בכל מאד.

[285] See Kli Yakar on Deuteronomy 31:17— השב מאהבה משיב גם אחרים כי האוהב את המלך רוצה שהכל יאהבוהו.

[286] R' Moshe Wolfson introduction to Shabbat page 38 where he also attributes this to the custom of having a *tisch*.

[287] Perhaps that is why the Psalm for Shabbat, 92, includes "all evildoers are scattered". Shabbat has the ability to bring the good in people out, while also shedding the negative aspects of those same people.

another, as one loves themselves,[288] brings the love of God to the other,[289] loving God also brings us closer to each other.[290]

This dynamic exists between us and Shabbat as well. Shabbat is called an אות [291]—a sign or covenant. An אות connects two people or things. This is reflected in the letter ו—*vuv hachebor*—the conjunction "and" that connects the first and last letters of the Hebrew Alphabet together: אות.[292] The word "אות" also means "letter" and is a reminder that each one of us has a special connection to a particular letter in the Torah.[293] Without us, the Torah and this world are incomplete.

On Kol Nidre we take out all of the Torahs from the ark, and ask forgiveness from them, for falling short in our relationship. Knowing that we are worthy of the gift of Shabbat, and the Torah, can take effort to internalize, despite it being an explicit verse:[294] "כִּי אֲנִי יְהֹוָה מְקַדִּשְׁכֶם כִּי אוֹת הִוא בֵּינִי וּבֵינֵיכֶם לְדֹרֹתֵיכֶם לָדַעַת"—for this Shabbat is a sign between Me and you, throughout the ages, that you may know that I have made you holy."

To know something—לָדַעַת—is also a form of connectivity, like when Adam "knew" Eve— וְהָאָדָם יָדַע אֶת־חַוָּה.[295] We embrace this intimacy during the blessing of Kiddush when we bear witness and say וְשַׁבַּת קָדְשְׁךָ בְּאַהֲבָה וּבְרָצוֹן הִנְחַלְתָּנוּ—"You sanctified us through

---

[288] Leviticus 19:18.
[289] See Sfas Emes 643 *Parshat Kedoshim*.
[290] See Hachel HaBracha Deuteronomy 6:5 that "loving God" equals "loving neighbor".
[291] Exodus 31:17.
[292] Toras HaRemez page 216.
[293] See Megaleh Amukot Va'etchanan 186:1.
[294] Exodus 31:13.
[295] Genesis 4:1.

Your love by sanctifying Shabbat." It is on us to feel that love, and if we don't, to set that as a new goal and destination.

It is often really hard to truly believe that we are good, pure, and holy. Part of our preparation for Yom Kippur is to check in on our connection to ourselves, through the Shabbat, to receive it as a sign—אות—of how we are feeling on a spiritual plane. If on this Shabbat we are not feeling inspired by a deep sense of belonging, then we need to return to that loveable space of self. That is a fulfillment of *teshuvah m'ahava*—returning from a desire for love.[296]

---

[296] See עולת שבת תשנ"ט for why the first "return" is singular.

Canceling Sins, Not People

God is everywhere, all of the time, for all people. Consequently, we can always engage with God wherever we are, physically or spiritually. מִן־הַמֵּצַ֥ר קָרָ֗אתִי יָּ֑הּ עָנָ֖נִי בַמֶּרְחָ֣ב יָֽהּ—"From dire straits did I call upon God, God answered me with expansiveness".[297]

The Tur, a precursor to the Code of Jewish Law, begins the section on Yom Kippur preparations by instructing each person to commit, in their hearts, to appease and make amends with anyone who they might have hurt. He goes on to explain that the Day of Atonement doesn't help our interpersonal transgressions until we have first sought forgiveness from each other.

Although every sin בין אדם לחבירו—"between us and our friend" is a sin בין אדם למקום—"between us and God", because God commanded us not to treat people badly, tradition teaches that part

---

[297] Psalms 118:5.

of our individualized repentance process is found in the re-humanizing of people.

On the first Yom Kippur, when the Israelites were in the desert, we received forgiveness for the sin of the golden calf, and accepted the second set of Tablets. The giving of the Torah at Mount Sinai, and the first set of the Ten Commandments, required the unity of the entire nation.[298] The same condition remains true today. We must come together to be worthy of the holiness of this day.[299]

The source for the Tur's teaching is found in Perkie D'Rebbe Eliezer[300] who explains that the *Satan*, the accuser against the Jewish People, will litigate whether we are really behaving like the angels that we are expected to emulate, on Yom Kippur. One of the ways that we are judged, in comparison to the angels, is if there is peace between us the way in which there is peace in Heaven among them.[301]

In the mystical tradition in particular, there is a great emphasis placed on feeling connected to humanity, as limbs of the same body. The Ari Z"l taught[302] that if someone is in pain or suffering, everyone must join, with deep sensitivity, to that person's experience and pray on their behalf. It is perhaps for that reason that all of our personal confessions are always framed as part of the collective: "We have sinned".

---

[298] Exodus 19:2 and Rashi there.
[299] See the Munkatcher Rebbe 659.
[300] Chapter 46.
[301] See Rabbah Emunascha page 286.
[302] Beginning of the Gate of Kavanah on Morning Blessings.

We enumerate our sins in the structure of an alphabetical acrostic: "אָשַׁמְנוּ. בָּגַדְנוּ. גָּזַלְנוּ"—We have become guilty. We have betrayed. We have robbed…" They continue in the "*al chait*—עַל חֵטְא" as well, albeit in pairs. It is therefore noteworthy that the three times we interrupt with the chanting of "וְעַל כֻּלָּם"—For all these, O God of forgiveness, forgive us, pardon us, atone for us" are not evenly spread out through the twenty-two letters of the Hebrew Alphabet. What is the intention in their placement after the letters: ""י"", ""ע"", & "ת"?

The Chamra Tava posits that it is an allusion to a verse[303] that is dealing with the Yom Kippur service:

וְסָמַךְ אַהֲרֹן אֶת־שְׁתֵּי יָדָו עַל רֹאשׁ הַשָּׂעִיר הַחַי וְהִתְוַדָּה עָלָיו אֶת־כָּל־עֲוֺנֹת בְּנֵי יִשְׂרָאֵל וְאֶת־כָּל־פִּשְׁעֵיהֶם לְכָל־חַטֹּאתָם וְנָתַן אֹתָם עַל־רֹאשׁ הַשָּׂעִיר וְשִׁלַּח בְּיַד־אִישׁ **עִתִּי** הַמִּדְבָּרָה:

Aaron shall lay both his hands upon the head of the live goat and confess over it all the iniquities and transgressions of the Israelites, whatever their sins, putting them on the head of the goat; and it shall be sent off to the wilderness through a **designated/timely** person.

Rashi explains that a person of "עִתִּי" is simply someone who was prepared, in advance, for this task. An essential aspect of spiritual practice is to know that we are designated to contribute unique

---

303 Leviticus 16:21.

goodness to the world, and our entire lives have prepared us for each moment.

Among the strongest forces in opposition to us achieving our greatest potential is the lack of awareness we bring to the holiness of where we find ourselves.

וַיִּיקַץ יַעֲקֹב מִשְּׁנָתוֹ וַיֹּאמֶר אָכֵן יֵשׁ ה" בַּמָּקוֹם הַזֶּה וְאָנֹכִי לֹא יָדָעְתִּי![304]

"Jacob awoke from his sleep and said, 'Surely God is present in this place, and I did not know!'"

On Yom Kippur, the High Priest would enter into the holiest place in the world, the Holy of Holies. This spiritual service wasn't just about access on Yom Kippur, but it assists in developing a year-round sensitivity to the holiness of space. When God first encounters Moses, by the burning bush, God tells him to take off his shoes because הַמָּקוֹם אֲשֶׁר אַתָּה עוֹמֵד עָלָיו אַדְמַת־קֹדֶשׁ הוּא, "the place upon which you are standing is holy ground."[305]

The Chafetz Chaim explains the verse as a charge, to each one of us, that "wherever we find ourselves, that is a place which we can sanctify through our action". We bring special attention to this by the Chazan reciting "HaMelech" from their place, in the congregation, instead of from the *bima* like every other prayer.[306]

Sefer Yetzirah, the Book of Creation, teaches that every experience of holiness is comprised of the three variables of "עולם שנה נפש—

---

[304] Genesis 28:16.
[305] Exodus 3:5.
[306] Rav Wachman.

place, time, and people".[307] The Divine Revelation alludes to this in the verse וְהַר סִינַי עָשַׁן, "and Mount Sinai was in smoke".[308] This smoke is also part of the offering of Yom Kippur, where the deeds of everyone, everywhere, for the whole year are brought before God.

Kidusha, the climatic communal prayer during the repetition of the *shmonie eshrie*, of Shabbat *musaf* quotes the angels מְשָׁרְתָיו שׁוֹאֲלִים זֶה לָזֶה אַיֵּה מְקוֹם—The Tanya explains that the angels are expressing their jealousy of our ability to access God, outside of heaven.

How can angels look up to us if we are looking down on each other?

One of the distinguishing features of angels is that they are spiritually stagnant. They don't struggle or grow. Their existence is inextricably linked to their designated purpose and they, unlike us, don't have the free will to choose who they are.

Repentance reinforces our belief that we can change for the good and be better. Seeing and supporting those opportunities in others helps return the world to a holier place and changes, not cancels, the culture.

---

[307] The first letter of each word forms עשן—smoke.
[308] Exodus 19:18.

Newark ICE Protest[309]

Good afternoon. I'm Rabbi Mike Moskowitz, my pronouns are he/him, and I'm here on behalf of CBST because we, like God, love immigrants. Our people were all strangers in strange lands and we know what happens when people are silent. These atrocities are the evil schemes of the few, but we are all responsible. When we say never again, we mean never again for everyone.

In these 10 days of Repentance, this time between Rosh Hashanah, the Jewish New Year, and Yom Kippur, the Day of Atonement, we make an accounting of our actions, and inactions, as individuals and as a community. We are here because we need to be able to answer

---

[309] This speech was delivered as part of an act of civil disobedience outside of an ICE complex in Newark, NJ in October of 2019. In entering my plea to the court I wrote "I was protesting the inhuman and immoral detention of people by ICE. As a Jew, as an American, and as a person, I feel encumbered by the dehumanization of others and called to disrupt those systems of oppression."

the One Who Created us all, equally in God's image, when God asks: "How did you let them do this to my children?"

How can we stand before the Master of the Universe on the Day of Judgment, and ask for mercy when we are complicit in this horrific cruelty? How can we have the audacity to cry out *Avinu Malkeinu*, Our Father our King, while we ignore the cries of God's children that we separated from their parents. If we want to be in relationship with God as a parent, we must see each other as siblings and this is not how you treat family.

Although NYC is a sanctuary city, as is Newark, immigrants who are stopped for minor traffic violations or other reasons in NYC, and then detained, actually get sent across the river and held here in NJ. The Essex County Detention Center holds immigrants under horrific conditions with widespread abuse, for profit. The LGBTQ community is particularly targeted because this is where fear, hate, and discrimination unite to exploit the perceived "other".

But there is no "other" in God's eyes. We just observed Rosh Hashana, celebrating the creation of the first person. The Talmud teaches that although God created all plants and trees, each according to their kind, and all the birds, fish, and animals, each according to their kind, God only created one person, in order to teach us the simple lesson that we still refuse to learn: that there are no "other" kinds of people.

Zecher Yetziat Mitzrayim, remembering the exodus of Egypt isn't a function of not forgetting, but of being able to recognize it in order to prevent it from ever happening again. We were enslaved, we were oppressed, and we were dehumanized. We have seen this all before.

Remembering, in our tradition, is a call to action. It is how we demonstrate that we have learned from our mistakes and will act differently in the future. It is on us to make it better. Never again is now!

Being Fully Present

A lot has happened in the Jewish calendar during the last two weeks since Rosh Hashanah, when we celebrated the birthday of the world. The Ten Days of Repentance, Tzom Gedialia, and Yom Kippur have guided us, along with the phases of the moon, from an initial, delicate emergence to a fuller, more embodied expression of self. Rosh Hashanah is described[310] as "לַיּוֹם חַגֵּנוּ בַּכֶּסֶה"—understood as the time when the new moon is essentially covered, כֶּסֶה. Today, on the fifteenth of the Hebrew month, the moon is fully exposed and now forms the סכה—sukkah.[311] It invites us to

---

[310] Psalms 81:4.
[311] See Rav Wolfson 659 Nitzavim.

uncover our hearts[312] and shine forth the most complete, wholesome, and beautiful version of ourselves.

This world, we are taught, is sustained by three things: עַל הַדִּין וְעַל הָאֱמֶת וְעַל הַשָּׁלוֹם—on judgment, truth, and peace.[313] The Kamarna Rebbe[314] explains that these three quantities correspond to the festivals of Rosh Hashanah, Yom Kippur, and Sukkot. Although the holiday of Sukkot only lasts about a week, we ask God throughout the year to וּפְרוֹשׁ עָלֵינוּ סֻכַּת שְׁלוֹמֶךָ, "shelter us with a sukkah of peace".[315] What then is the special opportunity now, that we are uniquely able to access?

As a structure that is intended to provide shelter, the sukkah has some odd parameters. *S'chach*, the covering that forms the roof and provides the most distinguishing feature of a sukkah, must offer more shade than sun, while still being loose enough to observe the stars through the gaps. It is certainly not meant to prevent rain from coming in, and it only requires two and a half walls to qualify. Not particularly robust requirements for a building that is intended to provide safety and peace.

We know our real sense of security isn't provided for by physical coverings, like a blanket or locks on a door, but is connected to the trust we place in the ultimate Protector, who doesn't sleep—שׁוֹמֵר יִשְׂרָאֵל.[316] This is also true in the relationships we have with people and places. We are constantly navigating what we share and with

---

[312] The word lulav לולב is an anagram for לב לו—a call to reveal the goodness of one's heart. It is also an allusion to וְטַהֵר לִבֵּנוּ לְעָבְדְּךָ בֶּאֱמֶת.
[313] Pirkei Avos 1:18.
[314] In Notzer Chesed.
[315] See blessings after the Shema.
[316] Psalms 121:4.

whom. When we choose to reveal truths about ourselves, and how to assess who is worthy of that access. There is comfort in being in spaces that are reliably consistent. This world, "עוֹלָם" in Hebrew, is scary in part because of the hidden, "נעלם" aspects that make us feel vulnerable.

One of the special features of Sukkot is the Biblical direction to "take the product of *hadar*"—פְּרִי עֵץ הָדָר.[317] In the Talmudic discussion, exploring the meaning of this phrase, it teaches:[318]

פְּרִי עֵץ הָדָר: עֵץ שֶׁטַּעַם עֵצוֹ וּפִרְיוֹ שָׁוֶה—הֱוֵי אוֹמֵר זֶה אֶתְרוֹג.

> Fruit of a beautiful tree: a tree that the taste of its trunk, and the taste of its fruit are alike. You must say it is the *etrog* tree.

The mystics observe that with all other fruits, a byproduct of the tree, the qualities of its source, like the roots, are concealed.[319] The highlighted feature of the Etrog is its transparency of self, including where it is coming from.

This doesn't diminish its depth or fullness. Just the opposite. There are four concepts, where the Rabbis have found it necessary to add the word "complete—שלמה". "Faith" אמונה, "repentance" תשובה,

---

[317] Leviticus 23:40.
[318] Sukkah 35a.
[319] See Toras HaRemez page 226.

"healing" רפואה, and "redemption" גאולה are all followed by שלמה.
The first letter of each of these words forms אתרג—*etrog*.[320]

Being fully oneself invites others to do the same, without
competition. "Fruit of a beautiful tree—פְּרִי עֵץ הָדָר" is also
understood as "היינו הדר הכל"[321] a reality where everyone can be.
The collective can't be complete if people are not bringing their full
selves.[322] It is in this beauty of authentic communal inclusion where
God resides דר ה'.[323]

---

[320] The Machzor of Vitry sees and allusion to the 613 commandments in etrog:
" אתרוג בגימטריא שש מאות ועשר. ולולב והדס וערבה. הרי תרי"ג מצות ששקולה
מצוותו לפני המקום כתרי"ג מצות".
[321] Sefer HaBahir 173–175.
[322] The Bahir write: שעם כל אחד הוא ועם כולן יחד הוא.
[323] Zohar 1:220b:15.

Cheshvan

Struggling to Feel the Blessing[324]

Transgender Day of Remembrance is observed annually, on November 20, to honor the lives that have been lost to anti-transgender violence—may their memories be for a blessing. It is a day that is designated for internalizing our collective responsibility to protect the vulnerable and marginalized. If society better understood the trans experience as the holy gift that it is, then next year we would be celebrating the blessings of their lives being lived, not the memories of their lives lost.

The Hebrew word for blessing, ברך—*baruch*, evokes the idea of increasing our attachment to another. The three letters that form

---

the word have the numerical values of two, twenty, and two hundred; when we support each other, blessing multiplies.

Although being transgender is absolutely a blessing, for many the experience is overwhelmingly hard. The struggle to live authentically while one's identity is being questioned, debated, and legislated is not easy. Living under the constant existential threat of being erased is nothing to be grateful for; yet this is the story, and struggle, of the Jewish people.

In this week's *parsha* we read about how Jacob had to run away from home, fleeing his brother Esav. Esav wanted to kill Jacob because of Jacob's identity as the first born. And still, Toldot is known as the Torah portion of blessings. Each *aliyah* has blessings in it, with the word for "blessing" mentioned more here than anywhere else in the Torah.

The climatic blessing that Isaac gives to Jacob begins the sixth *aliyah*. Tradition teaches that the number six is always associated with blessing. This week's Torah portion is the sixth in the Book of Genesis, and the sixth *aliyah* begins with the sixth letter in the Hebrew Alphabet, the *vuv*—ו.

וְיִתֶּן־לְךָ֙ הָאֱלֹהִ֔ים מִטַּל֙ הַשָּׁמַ֔יִם וּמִשְׁמַנֵּ֖י הָאָ֑רֶץ וְרֹ֥ב דָּגָ֖ן וְתִירֹֽשׁ׃

And may God give you the dew of the heavens and the excess of the earth, and abundant grain and wine.   Genesis 27:28

The *midrash* explains that this blessing begins with the conjunction "and" to teach us that blessings are continuous and ongoing: "May God give, and give again". We acknowledge this, as King David wrote in Psalm 68:20, בָּרוּךְ ה' יוֹם יוֹם—"Blessed is Hashem, every day".

This letter *vuv* is known as the "*vuv hachibur*", literally "the *vuv* that connects", and is often understood in rabbinic literature as "וא"ו מוסיף והולך—the *vuv* adds and continues". The presence, or absence, of this letter speaks to a sense of growth and an awareness of the work that is still required to achieve completeness.

Jacob, when spelled with the *vuv*, "יעקוב", has a numerical value of 188, half of the value of the word "shalom", whose numerical equivalent is 376. Rabbi Meir Yechiel HaLevi, the Ostrovtser Rebbe, explains that this reflects Jacob's belief that he was only complete when he was helping another. His brother Esav's name, by contrast, has a numerical value of 376 by itself, demonstrating that his sense of fullness came only from separation and isolating himself from others.

Communities, and allies, can offer comfort, safety, and support to those feeling alone or invisible. As we remember those that this world has failed to protect, we must create more awareness of what is necessary to ensure it doesn't happen again. The word "*toldot*" also means an extension of a broader principle, as demonstrated in conversations about the laws of shabbat and in the *mishnayot* of ethics. It is not enough to hold generic truths about the value of human life. We must apply those beliefs to the moment by moment struggles of trans folks, particularly trans youth.

When the Israelites were displaced in the desert and beginning their recovery from being enslaved, God delivered manna each morning that was surrounded by dew to protect it. This was a fulfillment of Isaac's blessing "And may God give you the dew of the heavens". It also models for us that it isn't enough to provide, even in miraculous ways, sustainable access to basic needs and resources—they also must be protected.

This year will continue to present difficulties to the trans community and with it, ongoing opportunities to come together to elevate and alleviate the struggle. God tells Abraham "I will bless those who bless you and curse the one who curses you". The word for "blessing—ברכה" has the same numerical value as the word "remember—זכר". When we recall those who are no longer here, and are inspired because of them to make this world a better place, then their memories become a continued source of blessing for all of us.

Remembering Through Action[325]

Last year in honor of Transgender Day of Remembrance (TDOR), we wrote about mourning those we've collectively lost to anti-transgender violence. This year, we again mourn. At least 22 more transgender or gender non-conforming people have been killed and the overwhelming majority of those reported killed are Black transgender women. We say "at least" because all too often these deaths are unreported or misreported.

However, we must do more than just mourn and remember. We must do more than wait for each November 20th to acknowledge the lives of transgender people—particularly Black transgender women—after their lives have been cut short by hatred and violence. In the Jewish tradition, remembering is a call to action. We recall the pain of the past, lean into it, and commit to make

---

[325] Originally published for Keshet on November 11, 2019 and co-authored with Seth Marnin.

things better for the future. But how do we do that? How do we see what we don't recognize? How do we understand lives that are seemingly so different from our own?

It requires us to show up, be present, and lessen the suffering. In the words of Bryan Stevenson, we must get proximate to suffering and understand the nuanced experiences of those who suffer from and experience inequality. Stevenson believes that if you are willing to get closer to people who are suffering, you will find the power to change the world. But in order to get proximate, in order to show up, we must see who is suffering.

A theme of this week's *parsha*, *Vayera*, is seeing. The reading begins with Abraham seeing God and the three angels who deliver news of Sarah bearing a son. "Looking up, he saw three men standing near him."[326] Later in the reading, Hagar's eyes are opened by God in order to see the life-saving source of water. "Then God opened her eyes and she saw a well of water."[327] We also read the *Akedah*—the binding of Isaac—when Abraham sees the ram caught in the thicket that he will sacrifice, rather than his son. "When Abraham looked up, his eyes fell upon a ram, caught in the thicket by its horns."[328] Each instance of seeing required looking up, adjusting their vision in order to see what was before them.

Seeing can be difficult. It can be painful. Nearly every day, if we raise our eyes, we can see the suffering of those around us—and, unfortunately, there is no shortage. And when we do see the suffering, we want to lessen it. We want to help, we want to make it

---

[326] Genesis 18:1–2.
[327] Genesis 21.19.
[328] Genesis 22: 13.

better, and be kind. But we are often unsure how. Abraham models these acts of kindness in *Vayera* when he welcomes three men into his tent.[329]

These men were strangers, not his people, but "others." Despite being unfamiliar, he invited them into his home. In reality, these were angels in human form who needed nothing. His act of inviting guests into his tent was not a reaction to seeing people without a place to stay or food to eat, but because of the intrinsic desire to demonstrate compassion, as God had modeled for Abraham. His guests were only sent so that Abraham could manifest the hospitality shown to him by God.

God created and maintains this world with kindness, but we have allowed the world to be unkind. We have seen with our own eyes the suffering in our communities. We therefore must act and rebuild. We must honor those we have lost. We must redouble our efforts to change the environment that allowed these tragedies to occur. We must commit to getting proximate, to seeing the humanity of those who are unfamiliar to us. And we must pledge to center and elevate the transgender voices of the living, particularly the most vulnerable.

Our rabbis teach that each person is a microcosm of the world and to save even one person is to save the world. Although there is just one earth, the ways in which we experience and live on it are often so unrecognizably different that it really isn't the same world at all. On this Transgender Day of Remembrance, let us light a *yahrzeit* candle not only to remember those we have lost, but to guide us in

---

[329] Genesis 18:2–8.

bringing more kindness, more compassion, and more justice in this world. *Kein yehi ratzon.*

Turning Mourning into Action[330]

This Friday, November 20th, we will again observe Transgender Day of Remembrance. We will again read the names of those who were killed by anti-transgender violence this year. And again we must ask ourselves: how do we meaningfully honor their lives?

The Talmud explains that honoring those who are no longer with us involves more than simply refraining from actions that would disappoint them. Rather, in order to honor them, we must do something productive and effect change.

How can we ensure there are no more names on a memorial list? How can we work to create a world where we celebrate the contributions and presence of transgender people? How can we devote our efforts to creating a world where transgender people do

---

[330] Originally published for Keshet on November 17, 2020 and co-authored with Seth Marnin.

not need to fear for their safety or feel compelled to hide their identities in order to remain safe?

This week's *parsha* offers insight into answering these "hows". The consequences of feeling compelled to hide an identity are recounted in Toldot. We read that Isaac and Rebecca live in Gerar but do not feel safe revealing their relationship to the other residents. When the men of Gerar ask about Rebecca, rather than tell them that she is his wife, Isaac lies and claims that Rebecca is his sister.[331] When Avimelech, King of the Philistines, realizes that they are in fact married, he confronts Isaac. Isaac explains that he had been afraid that the truth about Rebecca's identity as his wife would get him killed.[332]

Avimelech makes it clear that Isaac's inability to be candid about Rebecca's identity is dangerous for the community. The king worried that the community would act inappropriately because they misconstrued her relationship to Isaac. Addressing Isaac's fears, the king threatened the people of Gerar with death if they harmed Isaac or Rebecca.[333] The results of Avimelech's advocacy were immediate and miraculous. Isaac and Rebecca thrived.[334] They went from living in fear to flourishing in one verse. Avimelech's leadership not only created a safe space to acknowledge Rebecca's identity, but he used his power to change the dominant culture and can serve as a role model in this way.

So what lessons can we take away from this narrative? Everyone, but especially our leaders, can make an immediate and meaningful

---

[331] Genesis 26:7.
[332] Genesis 26:9.
[333] Genesis 26:11.
[334] Genesis 26:12.

difference in the lives of transgender people. It also tells us about the value of educating the community to respect authentic identities, and teaching the community members how to conduct themselves appropriately.

Here are some ways that we all can honor the lives of those we remember on Transgender Day of Remembrance:

Educate yourself.

- Take steps to educate yourself about transgender and non-binary people.
- Learn how to be supportive of someone who is trans and has come out to you.
- Learn about our obligation to respect name changes.

Make transgender lives visible and livable in our communities.

- Let us know we belong in your community.
- Share your pronouns. Create the space for others to share theirs, if they choose.
- Make sure that gendered spaces are inclusive of transgender people. Transgender women are women, transgender men are men. And work with nonbinary community members to ensure that there is space for them and their experiences.

Teach our community members how to be respectful.

- Be a *dugma*, an example, to your community.

- Have inclusive policies that are transgender affirming.
- Evaluate the forms, applications, and questionnaires your community uses to be sure they are inclusive.

Chaver up.

- Speak out as an ally in support of transgender people and transgender rights.
- Address the racism, ableism, misogyny, and other systems of oppression that are present in our communities.

The need to have a list of those we have lost on Transgender Day of Remembrance reflects our communal failure to value and protect all of God's children. Each of us can lead by example. We can be passive in our response to the violence and the names on the list. Or we can choose to change it. We must do everything within our power to ensure that there is no list next year.

Speaking Up for Trans Youth[335]

The new spate of anti-trans legislation restricting access to medical care and curtailing the ability to play gender-appropriate sports is devastating not only for trans folks but also for all Jews, as it strikes a blow at a core Jewish value: Do not cause distress by referring to a person's past identity. When lawmakers in Alabama, Arkansas, Tennessee, Mississippi, and South Dakota use the megaphone of their position to let trans folks know that they are reduced to the gender they were assigned at birth, these lawmakers are causing harm through verbal mistreatment of trans folks—especially trans kids—and those who love them, and they are attacking this essential Jewish principle.

---

[335] Originally published for Keshet on May 6, 2021 and co-authored with Jericho Vincent.

In this week's *parsha*, *Behar-Bechukosai*, we are instructed, "do not harm one another".[336] The Talmud explicitly uses this mitzvah as a foundation for a prohibition on bringing up the past when it will hurt people who have transitioned to a new identity,[337] which is further illustrated by the powerful story of Reb Yochanan and Reish Lakish.

When Reish Lakish, the head of a gang of bandits, encounters Reb Yochanan, a great Jewish scholar, he repents and becomes one of the greatest rabbis of the Talmud, as well as Reb Yochanan's best friend and brother-in-law. One day in the study hall, though, amidst an argument over the precise moment that a weapon becomes a finished product according to Jewish law, Reb Yochanan, perhaps cowed by Resh Lakish's opinion, makes a snide rejoinder: "A bandit knows about his banditry." Resh Lakish is so devastated to be identified and judged by an identity he long ago shed that he soon dies. Reb Yochanan is so distressed by the loss of his friend that he too dies.

What's strange about this story is that Reb Yochanan is actually a champion of the law against harming others. At an earlier point in the Talmud, he teaches that hurting someone through words is worse than damaging someone financially. And yet even he, a committed ally, causes great harm through his carelessness of speech.

---

[336] Leviticus 25:17.
[337] Bava Matzia, 58b.

What message are we sending to the trans folks in our communities, especially the trans kids, if we allow this new transphobic legislation to stand? As the poet Adrienne Rich wrote, "Lying is done with words, and also with silence." Have we told lies with our silence? Or have we defended our Torah, and let the world know that these transphobic attacks are attacks on Torah-true values?

The stakes could not be higher. Trans teens are at extraordinarily high risk of suicide. Research shows that the gender-affirming medical care denied by the latest legislation is associated with lifelong decreases in suicidal ideation. The ancient Rabbinic *midrash*[338] links this week's mitzvah of "Do not harm one another" to a line in Proverbs:[339] "Death and life are in the power of speech." Death and life are in the speech of these transphobic lawmakers and death and life are also in the speech of any Jewish leader brave enough to affirm the Torah-true principle of honoring people in their identities.

---

[338] Vayikra Rabbah 33:1.
[339] Proverbs 18:21.

Kislev

Increasing the Light of Allyship[340]

In a time of national identity searching, introspection and anticipation, Hanukkah can be an inviting space to reflect and refract the light before us. From the Hanukkah that was to the Hanukkah we arrive at, the world has shifted and we are not the same. This holiday of chocolate, oil and games of dreidel beckons us into a moment of contemplation.

Hanukkah expresses a language of novelty, innovation and a miraculous expansion beyond what we thought was possible. The ease and accessibility, the simplicity of candles, the sense that

---

[340] Originally published for the *Jewish Journal* on December 15, 2020 with Rabbi Dara Frimmer.

Hannukah is predictable and performative belies the very creative, radical nature of the Festival of Lights.

The annual Hanukkah experience, at its core, is an opportunity to receive new insight, empowerment and opportunity to overcome the forces that oppress, debase and deny our most essential identities. Had the few Maccabees not searched to provide that light for the many, none of us would have a miracle to celebrate today. Even though we are privileged to be able to publicly observe our traditions, Hanukkah reminds us that our work is not complete until everyone can safely and freely express their identities.

Visibility and Proximity

One of the unique aspects of Hanukkah is that it is the only festival that occurs in two different months. It is literally positioned between Kislev and Tevet to help us be aware and adapt to changing times. In the light of the candles, it is possible to see our roles anew, clarifying our commitment to ensuring that the privilege and expression of being is available to everyone.

When the Talmud explores modalities of the mitzvah of lighting the hanukkiah, it says that each and every person should have a candle. It continues to explain that an even greater beautification of the mitzvah is when everyone is able to increase the light with each additional day. When everyone has their own hanukkiah, when everyone is able to light all the candles on each night, then *everyone* is bringing the fullest light possible. This is the hope: with so much light, the world is relieved of darkness.

Our Rabbis teach that this attribute of adding is connected to Joseph, whose story we read on Shabbat Hanukkah. Joseph's name means to increase, and his story reveals the relationship between proximity and visibility. The Talmud,[341] juxtaposes the narrative of Joseph being thrown into a pit with the laws detailing the proper placement of the menorah and the limits on how far off the ground it can be:

In Genesis,[342] Joseph's brothers "saw [Joseph] from afar… and they conspired against him." They throw him into a pit, which Genesis 37:24 says "was empty and didn't have water." But the Rabbis disagree, arguing that while "empty" implies that the pit didn't have water in it, it was not without venomous pit-dwellers. There were snakes and scorpions that the brothers didn't know about, because they were not close enough to the pit to see.

Moreover, the distance at which the brothers first saw Joseph approaching made it easy for them to plot against him. In not one, but two cases, the brothers' lack of proximity led to actions that degrade and humiliate. If only they waited to see their little brother up close before acting, they might have changed their plan. If only they approached the pit to look inside, they might have seen the snakes and scorpions. The Torah is clear: Proximity and visibility lead to responsibility.

It is for that reason the Talmud instructs us that we cannot place a menorah too far off of the ground—we must be close enough to see and be affected by the Hanukkah candles. If the menorah can't be seen, we miss the message of the miracle, and the opportunity to take responsibility is lost.

---

[341] Shabbat 22a.
[342] 37:18.

The Hasmoneans were descendants of Aaron, who the Mishna tells us was a lover of peace, pursuer of peace and lover of peoples. Judaism is a religion of action, and we must be practitioners of our tradition's wisdom by taking responsibility.

Today, even with technologies that keep us connected across oceans and continents, we understand the challenge and, more so, the threat of being too distant. Jews have a response to prevent the dehumanization that often comes when we are distanced from the lived experience of others: Draw in close.

A Great Miracle Happens with Allyship

The Hebrew words behind the story of Hanukkah and Joseph also reaffirm the holiday's charge to increase visibility, to be an ally. The rabbis saw our world as created through speech and language, and thus, all Hebrew letters represent hidden truths. Just like the story of Joseph in the pit, the closer you look, the more that is revealed. The light of Hanukkah assists in the discovery.

The mystics teach that the Hebrew letters for Greece, יון, are three lines that descend as the word progresses. The great and mighty culture that claimed elite thought and refinement was in fact a culture that debased and denigrated. Greek leadership prioritized the body over the spirit. What was seen on the outside was of greater value than that which was within. Thus, it could be said that Greece, by elevating the external, actually debases it, a message hidden within the descending letters: יון.

The Hebrew word for Joseph, יוסף, begins with the same first two letters. But the third letter, though, is where the comparison is stark. Instead of a *nun* (ן) which is a straight line going down, we have a round *samech* (ס), a symbol for equality. Unlike the hierarchy of the *nun*, the circle of the *samech* allows every point on its circumference to be equidistant to the center. Joseph chooses to *chaver* up and stops the descent by treating others as equals.

The *nun* and *samech* form the word "miracle", נס. The first letter, *nun*, is the only letter in Hebrew that doesn't appear in the alphabetical acrostic of Ashrei. Our rabbis explain that this letter stands for "*nefela*," falling, and therefore is omitted. The next letter in the alphabet is the *samech* and starts the Ashrei verse, "*samech l'chol hanoflim*", "supporting all those who have fallen". Jews in those days, as in ours, had a choice between the *nun* and the *samech*—to align with the oppressors and feel secure or to ally with those who needed support. In choosing the latter, a great miracle (נס) happened there.

Kindling the Light of Hanukkah

As the story and words of Hanukkah convey, the Jewish response to oppression is not just to be free but to dismantle the system of oppression and provide equality for others. Today, we place a menorah in the window in order to publicize our engagement in the ancient and ongoing story of this struggle. We stand up in broken places of despair and hopelessness to rededicate ourselves and our institutions to this cause. Now, when we see an injustice, when we are proximate to the dehumanization of a child of God, we not only see the unholy act itself but also we recognize the imperative to respond.

This Hanukkah, kindle the light of liberation, not just for you and your loved ones, but for all people whose freedom of expression is threatened. Kindle a light to banish the darkness of hatred, racism, transphobia and misogyny. Kindle a light that signals to outsiders that you are a home (or an organization) committed to rededication and the recreation of holy space, particularly in the most broken of places.

Hanukkah was not immediately established as a holiday. The Talmud teaches that the Rabbis waited until the following year to institute a permanent commemoration. When they realized that the miracle could be replicated—that in every generation Jews could learn to take the little they had and turn it into something miraculous—they created the holiday. That is the holy ask of Hanukkah: to be the light that can extend and expand, to be the miracle that someone else needs.

Michael Walzer writes that "wherever we go, it is eternally Egypt," but that there is a Promised Land and the only way to make it across the wilderness is by "joining hands, marching together." The story of oppression and liberation is also a story of allyship. We will not survive without hands to support and guide us, to hold and elevate us. This year, on Hanukkah, be the light and bring the light out of the closet and into the world.

Tevet

Joseph's Journey from Forced Migration to Redemption: A Model for Immigration Justice[343]

He was not like the other boys. While they went out to the fields he stayed behind, curling his hair and kohling his eyes.[344] He walked with a lilt[345] and wore a colorful coat that caught everyone's attention.[346] He was a dreamer. The other boys hated him and could not even bring themselves to utter a friendly word in his

---

[343] "Joseph's Journey from Forced Migration to Redemption: A Model for Immigration Justice" by Rabbi Sharon Kleinbaum and Rabbi Mike Moskowitz from *Social Justice Torah Commentary*, edited by Rabbi Barry H. Block. Copyright © 2021 by Central Conference of American Rabbis. Used by permission of the CCAR. All rights reserved.
[344] B'reishit Rabbah 84:7. 2.
[345] B'reishit Rabbah 84:7. 2.
[346] Genesis 37:3.

direction.[347] One day their hatred grew so intense that they tore off his clothes and sold him into slavery, at just seventeen years old.[348] This began Joseph's forced migration down to Egypt,[349] and it ultimately led to our national enslavement.[350]

In our contemporary world of social justice, we often place different struggles in separate silos, imagining that somehow they exist in isolation. We assume that the struggle for the full equality of LGBTQ people is separate from the struggle for immigrant rights and protections. The Torah never makes this mistake. And in *Parshat Vayigash*, the interweaving is powerful. LGBTQ people are among the immigrants who struggle for asylum and refugee status and are also among the refugees who flee from violence and persecution. Economic collapse is a truth for all, regardless of sexual orientation and/or gender identity. And those who are LGBTQ and/or gender nonconforming face an even greater burden as immigrants.

At Congregation Beit Simchat Torah, the largest LGBTQ synagogue in the world, we collaborate with the New Sanctuary Coalition of NYC, SAFE, and RUSA LGBT to offer a pro se legal clinic for immigrants. Our clinic supports immigrants from all over the world, 75 percent of whom are LGBTQ and/or HIV-positive, making ours the only clinic with this special focus. We welcome and work with immigrants for any reason. Dozens of synagogue

---

[347] Genesis 37:4.

[348] Genesis 37:2.

[349] Genesis 37:23–28.

[350] The intergenerational trauma from the sale of Joseph is attributed as the cause of the ten martyrs.

volunteers and a small staff have dedicated their resources to supporting and expanding these efforts.

Our Rabbis understand Joseph as a person who stood out from his brothers and suffered greatly from their unwillingness to accept him as he was. His experience resonates with many LGBTQ folks who are forced from their homes and made to travel to foreign places in dangerous conditions, reflecting the complicity of a society that enables these atrocities.

Joseph's position upon arrival in Egypt is precarious. The *midrash* teaches that both his master, Potiphar, and his master's wife desire Joseph and plot to sexually abuse him.[351] He is alone, vulnerable, and eventually imprisoned for trying to defend himself. Yet despite his hardships and suffering, Joseph perseveres, becomes the viceroy of Egypt, and reinvests in healing and advancing the relationships with his brothers.

Although Joseph is dehumanized and expelled, he rallies, exceeding all expectations to navigate climate change and the subsequent food insecurities, while saving Egypt and his family of origin.[352] His Hebrew name, Yosef, alludes to these two roles: to add on and to gather together.

It is perhaps because he is born into cycles of displacement[353] and humiliation[354] that he is so committed to ending it. Joseph's ability to prioritize human dignity, unity, and forgiveness over hate, division, and fear produces the first set of biblical siblings who are

---

[351] Babylonian Talmud, Sotah 13b.
[352] Genesis 41:54.
[353] Rashi 37:2: "Everything that happened to Jacob happened to Joseph.".
[354] Genesis 30:23.

able to get along with each other.[355] It is one of the reasons that we have a custom to bless our children as Joseph's children were blessed.[356]

In chapter 45 of Genesis, Joseph finally comes out to his brothers, revealing his identity while modeling restorative justice and rehabilitation of society. Because the brothers have never been open to seeing Joseph as an equal, they're unable to recognize him when he is talking to them from a position of power.

Only when the pain of staying silent outweighs the pain of screaming out does Joseph finally give voice to his internal turmoil. With tremendous sensitivity and deep empathy, he removes everyone else from the room and communicates his humanity to them in the universal language of crying.[357]

In one of the most intense moments in the Bible, Joseph simultaneously reveals, rebukes, and rebuffs the brothers' false claims of innocence and equality by saying, "I am Joseph—is my father [really] alive?"[358] The brothers have claimed to be preoccupied with the well-being of their father and how Jacob couldn't possibly survive being separated from his son Benjamin, so here they are reminded that they didn't seem to care at all about

---

[355] Their mother, Asenath, also had a traumatic background; she was born through the rape of Dina (Pirkei D'Rabbi Eliezer 48).
[356] Traditionally, boys are blessed in accordance with words that Jacob speaks to Joseph's sons, Ephraim and Manasseh: "By you shall [the people of] Israel give [their] blessing, saying, 'May God make you like Ephraim and Manasseh'" (first found in the siddur of Rabbi Jacob Emden).
[357] Genesis 45:1–2.
[358] Genesis 45:3.

their father when they sold Joseph and then crassly asked Jacob to identify Joseph's unique outfit.[359]

אֲנִי יוֹסֵף הַעוֹד אָבִי חָי

I am Joseph is my father still alive?[360]

The Rabbis see these five words as challenging our confidence in our own choices. If Joseph, among the youngest of the brothers, leaves them with no way to respond for their actions,[361] how are we going to answer those who will introduce themselves to us as "one of the children you put in cages"?

It is not the responsibility of people we have separated from their children, denied asylum, or kept captive in exploitative conditions to educate, support, or forgive us. But that is the role Joseph takes with his oppressors. As a corrective reaction to their "[seeing] him in the distance and . . . wickedly plotting against him to bring about his death",[362] Joseph invites them to "come, draw near to me",[363] engaging them in a way that makes it easiest for them to be receptive.[364]

Joseph then reviews with them the fact-based history of what happened—and, with excessive encouragement, he actually helps them process it.[365] Unfortunately, this absurdity is often observed

---

[359] Genesis 37:32
[360] Genesis 45:3
[361] See Genesis 45:3, "But his brothers were unable to answer him.".
[362] Genesis 37:18.
[363] Genesis 45:4.
[364] Rashi on Genesis 45:4.
[365] Genesis 45:5.

when privileged people feel encumbered by their own entitlements and need to be reassured of their own self-worth.

None of this, however, absolves the brothers of their actions nor the need to make amends for the communal impact. There is a curious moment in the brothers' reunion when Joseph gives each one a change of clothing, but he gives Benjamin four additional sets of clothing plus three hundred silver pieces (Genesis 45:22). The Vilna Gaon explains that the three hundred silver pieces are a form of reparations for Benjamin—who, due to Joseph's absence, had to work harder.[366] Even though this was by no means Joseph's fault, he teaches his brothers the importance of trying to make the community whole.

Many commentators are surprised that Joseph seems to favor Benjamin with extra clothing in the same way that Jacob earlier favors Joseph with a splendid coat.[367] They explain that Joseph is demonstrating his confidence in his brothers' rehabilitation. Judaism defines repentance as being in the same circumstances but responding differently. Although the brothers had initially been jealous of Joseph's special clothing, Joseph knows that they have changed and will not resent Benjamin's extra garments.

As Joseph sends the brothers home to retrieve their father, he warns them not to fight during the journey.[368] The *midrash* explains that Joseph is worried that the brothers will spend time arguing about who was to blame for Joseph's sale and, in so doing, lose sight of the larger goal of family reunification. Today as well, we

---

[366] Meir Yechiel Halevi Halstock, Or Torah haShalem, Vayigash, 257, based on Rashi.
[367] Babylonian Talmud, Megillah 16a.
[368] Genesis 45:24.

must take care not to allow factional infighting to distract us from achieving our dream of a just society.

Like Joseph, many LGBTQ immigrants seeking asylum in the United States make their journey alone. Today, Joseph is a young gay man from Russia whose parents and siblings have disowned him, with a plane ticket and $100 in his pocket, thanks to a tiny organization that helped him leave behind the daily fear that he might be beaten or killed. Today, Joseph is a transgender woman from Chechnya whose cisgender partner managed to scrape together money for a plane ticket to get her to safety; however, because they are not legally related, they have no path to living together safely in either country. Today, Joseph is a gay woman from a small village in Nigeria who has never heard the acronym LGBTQ, but who spent years trying to understand why she was constantly being attacked and beaten for wanting to live with her best friend instead of marrying a man.

Like our ancestor, today's Josephs are fleeing violence and rejection by families of origin, traveling and navigating new systems, often in a new language. They may have families of choice but very rarely have access to any legal documentation of those relationships from the countries they leave behind; they are much more likely to go through the months or years of applying for asylum alone. Everyone loses when we deny people the ability to be and to contribute. We, like the brothers, must atone for our actions and inactions by following Joseph's model, coming together to create the opportunities for all people to have their dignity restored and preserved.

Shvat

Winter of Our Redemption[369]

Justice is rarely calm. As the Egyptians retrench themselves in iniquity and race forward to recapture their Israelite slaves, God sweeps them into the raging waters of the sea. Rashi[370] explains:

כאדם שמנער את הקדרה, הופך העליון למטה והתחתונים למעלה, כך היו עולים ויורדים ונשברים בים

---

[369] Originally published for Bayit on January 17, 2022 and co-authored with Rabba Wendy Amsellem.
[370] On Exodus 14:27.

> Like a person stirring a pot, moving the top to the bottom and
> the bottom to the top, so were the Egyptians rising, falling, and
> breaking in the sea.

This image is a potent symbol of social justice. Raising the
oppressed frequently involves lowering the oppressors. Fixing
society requires shattering norms that reify injustice. We always read
the story of this final showdown with the Egyptians close to the
holiday of Tu B'Shvat.

Tu B'Shvat is described as *Chag Ha-Ilanot*, the Festival of the Trees.
However, the word "אילנות" doesn't appear anywhere in the Torah,
Prophets, or Writings. Although the Torah speaks a lot about trees,
the word generally used is עץ. The Rabbis observe that the
constellation of letters in "אילנות" only appears in one place in the
Bible, in the verse above, Exodus 14:27. Once the sea splits and the
Israelites are on dry land the verse says: וַיָּשָׁב הַיָּם לִפְנוֹת בֹּקֶר לְאֵיתָנוֹ—
the sea returned to its normal state/power. For trees as well, this is
a time of coming back to themselves. According to Rashi, this is the
day where the sap of a tree starts to rise up inside of itself.

This corrective resurgence is emblematic of the month of Shvat,
whose Mazel, or astrological sign, is the bucket (*d'li*). It must first be
lowered down in order to be able to draw up the water from the
well. Life is filled with downs and ups as part of the meaningful
struggle to be a healer in a broken world. Finding the balance of
productive effort, as opposed to the *avodot perech*/the work of
enslavement in Egypt, is alluded to in the role of the Tzadik, the

righteous whose light is invested in the future, represented in the letter צ which corresponds to the month.[371]

Our Rabbis[372] teaches that the wicked are initially at peace and later experience suffering. This may be because if one is in a place of privilege, and free from the need to struggle for oneself, one sins by not being proactive for others. The righteous, on the other hand, struggle at first and then are able to achieve and enjoy a better state of being. It is perhaps for this reason that Tu B'Shvat is the only one of the four Rosh Hashanas that is halfway through the month and not at the beginning, modeling the work that first needs to be done in order to be worthy of celebration.

According to the Ari Z"l, the 12 months of the year are reflected in the 12 possible permutations of the four letters of God's name י-ה-ו-ה— . Each month has a corresponding verse that follows the same order of those four letters in that month's permutation. The verse for the month of Shvat is הֵמֶר יְמִירֶנּוּ וְהָיָה־הוּא,[373] describing a sacrificial animal that has been improperly exchanged for another. The order of the letters in God's name, ה-ו-י-ה, are at first presented out of order, with the ה and י switching positions. The final two letters, ו and ה are presented in the correct order of God's name, alluding to the righting that happens in the middle of the month of Shvat.

Indeed, the correcting that occurs in Shvat has been preordained since Creation. Yalkut Shimoni[374] offers a different understanding

---

[371] Sefer Yetzera.
[372] Bereishit Rabbah 66:4.
[373] Leviticus 27:33
[374] On B'shalach 225.

of the phrase, וַיָּשָׁב הַיָּם לִפְנוֹת בֹּקֶר לְאֵיתָנוֹ—the sea returned to its original condition. The Hebrew word תנאי means a contingent condition. The *midrash* explains:

אר יונתן התנה הקדוש ברוך הוא תנאים עם הים שיהא נקרע לפני ישראל
הדא הוא דכתיב וישב הים" לפנות בקר לאיתנו [י"ד, כ"ז] לתנאו שהתנה
הקדוש ברוך הוא עמו

Rabbi Yonatan said, the Holy Blessed One made a condition [at creation] with the sea, that it would split for Israel, as the verse says, וַיָּשָׁב הַיָּם לִפְנוֹת בֹּקֶר לְאֵיתָנוֹ—the sea returned to its condition that God had stipulated.

This *midrash* is curious. Why does God make a condition with the sea? God is all powerful and could simply demand that the sea obey. The *midrash* asserts that God wants the salvation of Israel at the sea to be part of the natural order, not a sudden Divine intervention.

As soon as Israel walks through on the dry land, they become truly free and the Egyptians lose their power over them. The sea naturally then returns to its original strength. God programs this sequence of events into the natural order. Freedom will always lead to the disempowering of oppressors.

Earlier,[375] the Israelites looked up and saw the mighty Egyptian army, complete with horses, chariots and warriors, bearing down on them. They were trapped by the sea, with nowhere to run, and they

---

[375] Exodus 14:10.

were terrified. Their situation had never been more dire. As they explained to Moses, "it would have been better for us to be slaves in Egypt than to die here in the wilderness."[376] It was precisely at this dark moment, when they were too exhausted to visualize a path forward, that their ultimate salvation began.

Tu B'Shvat is a yearly celebration of this kind of moment. It always falls in the dead of winter, when the trees appear lifeless and vulnerable. Tu B'Shvat reminds us that even when we feel like we have nothing left in us, the process of regeneration and redemption may already have begun. When we reinvest in the fight for justice and equality, the disruption of systemic oppression will be as natural as the changing of the seasons.

---

[376] Exodus 14:12.

Adar

Ordering for Humanity[377]

On Purim we embrace the disorder of the ונהפוך הוא, *v'nahafoch hu*,[378] as a way of informing and preparing for the ideal reordering of society on Passover's *Leil Seder*, literally the night of order.

While on Purim we are meant to celebrate עַד דְּלָא יָדַע—"until we don't know the difference"[379] between "cursed is Haman" and "blessed is Mordecai"; on Passover we already know how to answer each child appropriately, and the questions that they will ask before they do.[380] We even extend our confidence to the significance of

---

[377] Originally published for Bayit on March 10, 2022.

[378] Book of Esther 9:1. Often translated as opposite or upside down.

[379] Megillah 7b.

[380] Esther, also called Hadassah, has the same numerical value as "know" = הדסה דע.

the order of numbers. We sing "Who knows one?" because we know what is first, and what comes next. Everything and everyone belongs, and knows its place.

In order to understand the best way to be, we must first acknowledge that we haven't yet figured it out. It is particularly in the external, finite spaces, that we are overly confident of what we think we know. We assume there are constraints[381] that prevent a sustainable model of universal coexistence and equality, but it is only our knowledge that has its limits.[382]

When Moses approaches the burning bush he can't understand how it isn't consumed.[383] God instructs him to remove his shoes as a way of indicating the physical constraints of interfacing with this world through the usual external tools. Moses, in recognizing that he "didn't know", merited to learn from the infinite.

Purim is a language of פרוד, separation, as Haman, a descendant of Amalek, describes the Jewish people as "עם אחד מפוזר ומפורד בין העמים"—a people separated and scattered among the nations. The verse hints that the essence of our identity is one of unity, being a nation of oneness, while acknowledging the reality of our current state of division. It is that disconnection that prevents us from knowing even that which is directly in front of us.

The Israelites are only in Egypt because Joseph's brothers hated him and exiled him through slavery. While Joseph was searching to

---

[381] Passover is זמן חרותינו—time of our freedom, and also when time is set free.
[382] The word for "until" is the same two letters as "knowing" (עד, דע).
[383] The bush, סנה has the same numerical value as לא ידע, not knowing. See תורת הרמז.

be one among his brothers,[384] אָחַי אָנֹכִי מְבַקֵּשׁ—they were jealous of him,[385] וַיְקַנְאוּ־בוֹ אֶחָיו—and certainly didn't treat him like family. A consequence of that othering was the inability to see him as their brother, both when they sold him and when they were reunited.

In *Midrash Rabbah*[386] we find that Joseph went to great lengths to reveal his identity, unsuccessfully. Despite his investment in organization, the brothers' commitment to their false narrative of a superior placement in the world prevented them from seeing what Joseph was trying to reveal to them.[387]

Ordering things, when they are not in conscious relationship with each other, is not revelatory:

> Joseph would strike his goblet and call out "Reuven, Simeon, Levi, Judah, Issachar, and Zebulun—sons of one mother, recline in this order—הסבו כסדר הזה, for it is the order of your births." So it was for all of the brothers. Once he reached Benjamin, he said "This one has no mother, and I have no mother. Let him sit next to me."

In the next verse the brothers continue to miss another *siman*, sign, laid out by Joseph:[388] "He passed portions from before him to them, and Benjamin's portion was greater than the portions of all of them; fivefold. They drank and they imbibed with him." The

---

384 Genesis 37:16.
385 Genesis 37:11.
386 92:5.
387 This is similar to when he shared his dreams with them as a teenager.
388 Genesis 43:33.

Talmud,[389] concerned how Joseph could repeat the act of his father by favoring one of them through clothing, explains that he intimated to Benjamin that his descendent [Mordecai] would go out before the king in five royal garments.[390]

Focusing on the externality of humanity internalizes, and reinforces, our prioritization of the superficial and restrictive aspects of people. Our rabbis teach[391]—נִכְנַס יַיִן יָצָא סוֹד—when the wine goes in, the [essential] secret [of self] comes out. The סוֹד of the Pardes—פרדס,[392] now emerges and leads the order of the seder—סדר.[393]

On Purim, we hide who we are by wearing costumes. Disguises also allow us the freedom to reveal who we really are. Covering what is usually revealed can express what is generally concealed. We observe the miraculous, that is concealed in a natural way, to change the nature of the mundane.[394]

When we recline and drink on *leil seder*, our embodiment of communal responsibility, unlike the brothers, provides the clarity and wisdom to know our place is in partnership with God and all of

---

[389] Megillah 16b.

[390] Esther 8:5.

[391] Eruvin 65a "יַיִן". אָמַר רַבִּי חִיָּיא: כָּל הַמִּתְיַישֵּׁב בְּיֵינוֹ—יֶשׁ בּוֹ דַּעַת שִׁבְעִים זְקֵנִים. נִכְנַס יַיִן—יָצָא סוֹד. Rabbi Ḥiyya נִיתַּן בְּשִׁבְעִים אוֹתִיּוֹת, וְ"סוֹד" נִיתַּן בְּשִׁבְעִים אוֹתִיּוֹת. said: Anyone who remains settled of mind after drinking wine, and does not become intoxicated, has an element of the mindset of seventy Elders. Wine was given in seventy letters, as the numerological value of the letters comprising the word is seventy. Similarly, the word "secret" was given in seventy letters.

[392] The Torah is understood to hold four planes of meaning: Peshat, Remez, Drash, and Sod.

[393] The "Sod-hidden foundations" is repositioned from the end of the "Pardes" to the beginning of the "seder".

[394] The angel of the month of Adar is אברכיא"ל which has the numerical value of סדר, order. See סודי רזי.

God's creations. As we are declaring "anyone who is hungry, let them come and eat", we should be bothered that the uniqueness of this declaration is a manifestation of our self-imposed limitations of the ideal to just this moment; and we should question it.

When we ask, "Why is this night different from all other nights" we shouldn't have a good answer. Perhaps it should be read as a rebuke and call to action. Maybe the Haggadah is asking us "Why does this night need to be different from all other nights?" It should not be. We must always welcome the hungry, express our gratitude to God, and appreciate the freedom affirming structures of our lives. When it comes to human rights and an equitable society, the things that make us different don't make a difference.

Atoning for the Spiritual Abuse of Conversion Therapy[395]

This week, I returned from the Global Interfaith Commission of LGBTQ lives, held in London, England. We met with human rights experts, medical professionals, and clergy. We heard firsthand accounts of the torturous nature of conversion therapy. With overwhelming evidence, they confirmed what we all already knew; that while this fear driven practice doesn't assist in actually changing a person's gender identity or sexual orientation, it is harmful and highly effective in converting people out of religion.

More countries, including Israel and Canada—and two dozen states in the U.S.—have made the malpractice of conversion therapy illegal. Yet, it still remains for religious communities, and especially the rabbis who lead them, to acknowledge and take responsibility

---

[395] Originally published for Bayit on March 29, 2022.

for those who have left our communities because of the homophobia and transphobia that we have created.

For too long rabbinic leadership has denied the trauma inflicted on LGBTQ people by our communities, exempting themselves from engaging in a conversation by hiding behind the effortless excuse of "what can we do, there is Leviticus 18:22?" This verse doesn't provide cover for a rabbi who tells a young gay man to marry a woman (who doesn't know that he is gay) because "How do you know you aren't attracted to women when you have never even been with one?" Or to tell a crowd gathered to hear words of Torah that "9/11 happened because we aren't protesting enough against the gays." It certainly does nothing to justify the dehumanizing request by a rabbi to ask a father not to bring his son, who is trans, to shul because it makes "people" uncomfortable.

Reading *Parshat Parah* this past Shabbat, we learned about the redemptive ritual of the red heifer, which was able to לטהר טמאים ולטמא טהורים, purify the impure and make impure the pure. The red heifer had to be תְּמִימָה אֲשֶׁר אֵין־בָּהּ מוּם אֲשֶׁר לֹא־עָלָה עָלֶיהָ עֹל without blemish, in which there is no defect and on which no yoke has been laid.[396] The Chozeh of Lublin sees this description as not only applying to the cow, but also to the moral awareness of human beings. He teaches that we need the red heifer to atone for those who see themselves as perfect and free from sin, but this is only because they don't feel the responsibility of the yoke of Torah. The lack of the awareness of our own deficiencies, and accountability to be responsible for others, is a source of the impurity. We must acknowledge that our perverse desire to label God's queer children

---

[396] Numbers 19:2.

as an abomination is a source of our own impurity that requires us to repent and cleanse ourselves from this unholy hatred.

It is this particular impurity that we, as the Children of Israel, are destined to fight. Esav is described as וַיֵּצֵא הָרִאשׁוֹן אַדְמוֹנִי כֻּלּוֹ כְּאַדֶּרֶת שֵׂעָר וַיִּקְרְאוּ שְׁמוֹ עֵשָׂו—The first one emerged red, all of him was like a hairy mantle, so they called his name Esav.[397] Two verses later Jacob is called תם—perfect and wholesome. The Chamra Tava connects the redness of the heifer to Esav, while the blemish-free nature resembles Yaakov. Thus, the eternal battle between Yaakov and Esav, between impurity and purity, is echoed in the red heifer.

Tradition teaches that the source of Esav's evil was his false sense of completeness (עשוי), he emerged first and saw himself as having already succeeded in the struggle. By contrast, Jacob who is assigned as the second child at birth, but identifies as the first born, has a lifelong transition. He begins as עקב, the heel, but after truly struggling and overcoming, he is called "Israel—ישראל" which can be parsed "לי ראש—my head".

In reference to the red heifer, King Solomon, the wisest of all men, said: כָּל־זֹה נִסִּיתִי בַחָכְמָה אָמַרְתִּי אֶחְכָּמָה וְהִיא רְחוֹקָה מִמֶּנִּי—"all of this I tested with wisdom, I thought I could become wise, but it is distant from me".[398] From a distance, it is impossible to understand the lived experiences of others and learn from them.

"Wisdom" doesn't produce the horrific track record of conversion therapy. Only a willful refusal to acknowledge the traumatizing pain it causes can explain this abuse. We told those who were pure that

---

[397] Genesis 25:25.
[398] Ecclesiastes 7:23.

they weren't. And many believed us. Many of those who were close, are now far away. And some are lost to us forever, אָדָם כִּי־יָמוּת בְּאֹהֶל.[399]

It will take much more than the acquisition of wisdom to purify the rabbinate for the iniquity of ריחוק, distancing people from God. All we can do is create opportunities for Kiruv, helping folks come close again. This Thursday, March 31, is Trans Day of Visibility. A day marked annually to celebrate the lives of transgender folks is such an occasion. We can learn, listen, and expand our ability to understand beyond the simple cerebral wisdom of the head, to the limitless care of the soul.

זֹאת חֻקַּת הַתּוֹרָה אֲשֶׁר־צִוָּה יְקֹוָק לֵאמֹר—This is the ritual law that God has commanded: Speak.[400] Ben Ish Chai learns from this verse that sharing the words of God requires being in conversation. We must be in relationship, up close and deeply personal. Dr. Mary McAleese, former President of Ireland, said at the conference: "People judge God by how people of faith live their lives and treat others." We must do away, once and for all, with the unholy practice of conversion therapy, cease this desecration of God's Name, and restore the dignity of LGBTQ people in religious communities.

---

[399] Numbers 19:14.
[400] Numbers 19:2.

Homophobia is the Real Abomination[401]

I received a call recently from an Orthodox man who knew that he was gay before he married his wife. "I think that God hates me because God made me gay," he said. Then he continued, "I was faithful for the first few years but now I've been with more men than I can remember and my wife still doesn't know." It is this man's internalized homophobia that causes him to agonize over a perceived "sin of being" instead of his actual deceit and disloyalty in cheating on his wife.

Leviticus 18:22 is the verse most often cited as declaring divine opposition to homosexuality. In that verse, the men of Israel are warned not to lie with other men as they do with women since that is a "*toeiva*". Although homophobic cultures project great certainty on the meaning of the word "*toeiva*", usually translated as "abomination", in the times of the Mishnah it was much less clear.

---

[401] Originally published for *The Times of Israel* Blog on March 4, 2020.

The Talmud[402] tells a story of Bar Kapara and Rebbe, the redactor of the Mishnah. Bar Kapara asks Rebbe, "What is the meaning of the word '*toeiva?*' Rebbe offers several answers and Bar Kapara rejects them all. Eventually, Rebbe asks what Bar Kapara thinks the word means. Bar Kapara explains: "תועה אתה בה", understood by the commentaries as "you are straying from your wife to be with another man."

We have further evidence that *toeiva* is connected to deceitfulness. In Deuteronomy,[403] *toeiva* is used to refer to those who possess unfair weights and measures. "For everyone who does those things, everyone who deals dishonestly, is abhorrent to the Lord your God." Just as God despises the duplicity inherent in presenting false weights as truthful, God does not want us to be deceitful in our most intimate relationships. By denying the existence of gay, lesbian, and bisexual folks, and forcing them into heterosexual relationships, we are the ones creating and enabling the *toeiva,* exactly as the Talmud understands the prohibition of Leviticus 18:22 to be!

This week we will read *Parshat Zachor*[404] and remember the treachery of Amalek, how they denied God's hand in the Exodus, and attacked God's people Israel. These verses immediately follow the description of the *toeiva* of false weights and further emphasize the severity of God's abhorrence of deception.

---

[402] Nedarim 51a.
[403] 25:16.
[404] Deuteronomy 25:17–19.

Being gay itself is not a *toeiva*. Forcing people to live a life of deception is.[405] It is indeed abhorrent and an abomination. Similarly, the Code of Jewish Law frames the prohibition of two women being together as an extramarital affair. It doesn't instruct mothers or teachers to inform young women about a prohibition but rather that husbands should warn their wives.

The horrific consequences of this communal failure are far-reaching. According to the Jerusalem Open House, new cases of HIV have increased in the *frum*, "hetero" community. It is well known in the non-Jewish gay community of Lakewood, NJ that one shouldn't date Jewish men, because they are likely married to women. As I'm writing this, another young Orthodox woman reached out asking for a *shidduch*, for a single *frum* woman, because she is tired of dating *Kollel* wives! Is this really what we think God wants from us?

There is no sin in being gay just as there is no mitzvah in being straight because both just are. No person today is forbidden to be. Now more than ever we must celebrate people being. Children of queer parents, parents of queer children, siblings, and friends are coming out and being allies, while staying in religious communities.

The question of LGBTQ equality in Orthodox spaces is a new one. Indeed, it is only relatively recently that non-Orthodox movements have become accepting of openly LGBTQ Jews. In those

---

[405] We also find this word in the prohibition of wearing misgendered clothing for licentious purposes. This is analogous to someone impersonating a doctor to gain access to patients. The revolting aspect obviously isn't being a doctor or dressing up as one, but rather the misrepresentation of self, to another, to gain access to intimate spaces.

communities as well, it was homophobia, not scripture that kept people out.

Being objective and separating out one's own prejudices and privileges is really hard. It is so much easier to keep and defend them through a false sense of piety. Esav, the source of Amalek, demonstrated this hypocrisy by asking his father how to tithe salt, while living a violent and immoral life. We are all suffering from the inherited trauma of religion and it is clearly influencing our relationships with others.

The flaws in our communities exist despite, not because of, biblical verses. Orthodoxy suffers from xenophobia even though there are dozens of biblical charges to love the stranger. If it was really about a verse, and not about feeling uncomfortable around those seen as different, would Jews of color and Jews by choice be so excluded from schools, dating, and leadership roles? Similarly, it is disingenuous to quote a verse to justify homophobia.

Our tradition is holy to the extent it helps us understand and fulfill the will of God. We don't serve commandments or verses, we serve God. The Talmud[406] (the Oral Law written down), quotes a verse, Exodus 34:27, that it is forbidden by scripture to write down the Oral Law. Rashi explains that there was a fear that Torah would be forgotten and so therefore it was justified to act accordingly and override the verse. If we are worried about Torah being lost, why aren't we worried about people being lost?

---

[406] Gitten 60b.

Our Rabbis explain[407] that the Jews not only accept the laws of Purim, but they also re-accepted upon themselves the entire Torah. Their first acceptance, at Mount Sinai, was out of fear. Here, as part of the Purim story, they accepted the Torah again, this time out of love. Remembering and eradicating the hate, fear, and deception of Amalek helps us prepare for the unifying love of acceptance.

---

[407] Esther 9:27.

Staying Safe on the Streets

According to the National Highway Traffic Safety Administration, over 20,000 people died in motor vehicle traffic crashes in the first half of 2022. That comes to approximately 100 people a day, being killed each day in this country. Additionally, each day brings with it an average of 7,500 injuries from car accidents. We use the word "accident" but as others have observed, it removes accountability from society. After all, it wasn't on purpose.

In preparation for the holiday of Purim we read a special selection, in addition to the weekly portion of Leviticus, known as *Parshat Zachor*, literally "remember". Contained in this section is the biblical obligation to "Remember what Amalek did to you on your journey".[408] After we left Egypt, during our 49-day journey to Mount Sinai to receive the Torah, Amalek attacked the Israelites.

---

[408] Deuteronomy 25:17

Haman, the evil villain of the Purim story, is a descendant of Amalek who also tried to destroy the Jewish people.[409]

These two readings elevate an intentional sensitivity to our encounters with others. "Vayikra" ויקרא means [God] called [Moses]. Rashi observes that unlike other words that introduce a conversation between God and Moses, like "said", "stated", or "commanded", "called" is one of affectionate connection. Rashi continues to contrast this holy thoughtful engagement with its similar sounding, but opposite and impure counterpart "Vayikar" ויקר, meaning to happen upon.

This is the same language that is used to describe Amalek's attack on us: "אֲשֶׁר קָרְךָ בַּדֶּרֶךְ" who chanced (unexpectedly) upon you along the way.[410] The *midrash* understand the root of this word, and it's source of evil, as "קר"—a coldness or apathy. It is this lack of reaction, to an unacceptable reality, that the Talmud attributes to the cause of the Purim story.

The Gemara[411] relates that the Jews of Persha were enjoying themselves at the festive party that King Achashveros hosted, and when the utensils of the Holy Temple were brought out to be used, the Jews were unresponsive. The acceptance of the defilement codes for the rabbis as more sacrilegious than the egregious act itself. Being complacent, in the face of injustice, denies the truth of our partnership with the Divine. Change is possible and we must work to achieve it.

---

[409] Megillah 11a.
[410] Deuteronomy 25:18
[411] Megillah 12a.

The mystical work of the Zohar identifies the role of false narratives in perpetuating the tragic status quo. He writes that the word for "lie" is שקר, and its operating system run on קר, a cold numbness. It is the claim that the world is random, chaotic, and unintentional that seeks to absolve us of responsibility and effecting change.

The numerical value of Amalek is 240, the same as *safek* ספק—doubt. When we are asked to contribute or respond to a need, we can attempt to deflect the obligation by simply stating that we are not sure if it will make a difference or question if the need is even real. In the Purim story the threat is eventually taken seriously and a total commitment to change motivates a shift in awareness, particularly in areas that could otherwise be ignored as insignificant. The *midrash*, for example, frames the verse where Mordechai hears all that has happened, כָּל־אֲשֶׁר קָרֶהוּ, as a deliberate communication and call to action.[412]

Remembering, in Jewish tradition, is always a call to action. Purim, named because of the lots that were thrown to determine the date of mass murder, reminds us that not paying attention is not an accident.

---

[412] Esther 4:7.

Reflecting the Greatness of Purim Katan[413]

The story is told of a person carrying a very heavy parcel standing by the side of the road. A wagon driver pulls up next to them and in an act of kindness offers the struggling person a ride. When the driver turns around to check on the passenger, they see that they are still exerting themselves holding the weight of the bundle above their head. "Why don't you put your burden down on the bench next to you?" the driver asks. "You were so generous and nice to give me a ride, I don't want you to have to carry the weight of my bag as well." The driver gently reassures the person, "Don't worry, I'm carrying you both already."

In order to be maximally effective as a person, and balance what often feels like the weight of the world on our shoulders, we need a clear understanding of what we ourselves are doing and what is being done for us. Knowing the source of our strength informs our

---

[413] Originally published for Bayit on February 14, 2022.

contributions to this world. Achieving this level of self-awareness, though, is not easy.

Indeed, encoded into the story of creation we have a description of the difficulty of properly perceiving one's agency:

וַיַּעַשׂ אֱלֹקִים אֶת־שְׁנֵי הַמְּאֹרֹת הַגְּדֹלִים אֶת־הַמָּאוֹר הַגָּדֹל לְמֶמְשֶׁלֶת הַיּוֹם
וְאֶת־הַמָּאוֹר הַקָּטֹן לְמֶמְשֶׁלֶת הַלַּיְלָה וְאֵת הַכּוֹכָבִים:

God made the two great lights, the greater light to dominate
the day and the lesser light to dominate the night, and the
stars.[414]

At first, the two luminaries are both described as "great lights." But by the end of the verse, one is declared greater and the other is called lesser. The Talmud[415] explains the shift:

אמרה ירח לפני הקב"ה רבש"ע אפשר לשני מלכים שיש תמשו בכתר
אחד?"

The moon said before God, "Is it possible for two kings to use
the same crown?"

The moon believed that it and the sun were being asked to share the title of "great lights." The moon argues that there should be a hierarchy. Unfortunately, the moon lacked the perspective and self-

---

[414] Genesis 1:16.
[415] Chullin 60b.

awareness to realize that it is simply reflecting the sun's light, so if only one of them is to be designated "great," it will be the sun.

The Talmud continues:

"אמר לה לכי ומעטי את עצמך"

God said to the moon: "Go and make yourself smaller."

The moon's preoccupation with power and influence blocked its own understanding of its role in the broader system. We are also illuminating forces, and we too need to be reminded that at our best we are a reflection of the Divine Light, and in partnership with God our greatness is limitless.

At the splitting of the sea during Nissan, the first month of the cycle of months, we witnessed the miracles and presence of God revealed. The Israelites pointed to God and said: עָזִּי וְזִמְרָת יָהּ וַיְהִי־לִי לִישׁוּעָה זֶה אֵ-לִי וְאַנְוֵהוּ God's strength and power to eradicate has been a salvation for me.[416] This is my God אֵ-לִי, and I will beautify God. אַנְוֵהוּ is also understood as an intimate coexistence; אני והו—I and God. Adar (א-דר), the last month of the year, supports our heightened awareness and reunification of God's presence, particularly when we are farthest from the source of God's revealed nature.

Esther, whose allusion in the Torah is from the verse וְאָנֹכִי הַסְתֵּר אַסְתִּיר פָּנַי בַּיּוֹם הַהוּא—I will keep My countenance hidden on that

---

day,[417] represents the Aleph, a reference to the Oneness of God, being dominantly expressed from within the hiddenness; א-סתר. With her true identity concealed, Queen Esther approaches the king, understanding that her life is very much on the line. As she gets closer, she is not concerned that she might fail in her attempt to save the Jewish people or end up dead like the previous queen, but her anxiety is focused on no longer having the companionship of God. The Bavli[418] teaches:

אָמַר רַבִּי לֵוִי: כֵּיוָן שֶׁהִגִּיעָה לְבֵית הַצְּלָמִים, נִסְתַּלְּקָה הֵימֶנָּה שְׁכִינָה. אָמְרָה: "אֵ-לִי אֵ-לִי לָמָה עֲזַבְתָּנִי"

Rabbi Levi said: Once she reached the chamber of the idols, the Divine Presence left her. She said: "My God, my God, why have You forsaken me?"

When King David feels powerless, he expresses it as כְּגֶבֶר אֵין־אֱיָל— literally as a person without strength, but the rabbis understand it as "as person feeling they are without אֵ-לִי".[419] Rav Chaver points out that the word ישראל is composed of the letters י-ש-ר-א-ל. What makes us an empowered nation is our relationship with God, conscious of our dynamic responsibility in it.

Giving proper attribution to the source of our power reminds us of the investment that God is making in sustaining us. The Talmud[420]

---

[417] Deuteronomy 31:18.
[418] Megillah 15b.
[419] Psalm 88:5.
[420] Bavli Bava Metzia 12b.

teaches in the name of Rabbi Yochanan: "גדול וסמוך על שלחן אביו זהו קטן—an adult that relies on their parents table is called a *katon*".

Purim Katan, which is completely dependent on Purim in the second Adar to exist at all, provides a gentle comfort in our pursuit of justice. Even in the darkest of times, we remember that with God's help anything is possible. All of us are small in relationship to God, and by fully acknowledging our dependence on Heavenly Assistance, we find the strength to continue journeying to try to make the world as God wants it to be, full of light.

Pride in the Ultra Orthodox Community Interview[421]

It is hard to imagine you as an Ultra Orthodox rabbi and a fierce advocate for LGBT+ rights. Which came first? Can you share a little bit about how the journey began?

You are right, this was not on the syllabus in Yeshiva. When I was first ordained, over twenty years ago, I never could have pictured this work as what I was preparing to do as a rabbi. Years later I found myself as a rabbi, at Columbia University and of the Orthodox synagogue in the neighborhood, when someone in my family came out as transgender.

In speaking to my own rabbis to find guidance and perspective, to try and gain some traction in understanding this identity, it became clear that they had never actually met someone of trans experience. There really weren't informed opinions, out there, on how to best respond and be supportive. So slowly, I started feeling more internal permission to think out loud and fill the void about these questions.

After many conversations, and then articles and speeches, it became more publicly known that I was someone who was trying to figure out ways to best offer approaches, within Jewish tradition, to the lived experiences of so many people that up until now, had simply been erased from the narrative of Orthodox Judaism. I came out,

---

[421] The AUJS Pod with Tanna and Parisa on September 19, 2022.

publicly, as an ally in a speech on Hanukkah, about six years ago. Since then I've published close to two hundred articles.

You used the term "coming out". Did it feel like that? Like you were "coming out" to the community?

Yes. It absolutely felt that way. And it wasn't clear to me that I was going to. As you know, many communities in the Orthodox world are not inviting or safe places for LGBTQ folks. I was writing under a pseudonym for about a year, for a wonderful organization called Keshet, because I didn't feel like I could write under my own name. When it became clear that I was the one writing those articles my employers told me to stop.

It wasn't a simple choice for me, at that moment. I needed to really think about if my faith was strong enough, in God and doing the right thing, to take on the precarity and deal with the consequences.

Have you faced any reactions from the non-Orthodox community?

The work that I do around trans issues is very broad and it involves a lot of interfaith and interdenominational spaces. There is a way in which it is so new, for most communities, even if they are supportive. For example: if you have someone who wants to convert to Judaism, was assigned male at birth, transitioned, and hasn't had bottom surgery. Does this woman need to go through circumcision, or *hatfas dam bris*? Is *bris milah* gender-specific or body part-specific?

These questions are complicated, in that they are new. Rabbis from all denominations reach out for support around rituals, name changes, and language to help move the conversation and communities to a better place. I also receive a lot of questions from clergy of other faiths that might not have the same concerns about other verses in the Hebrew Bible, wanting to understand better framings of the ones that are used to defend homophobia or transphobia.

There are increased conversations among many, who historically have been uninterested in exploring the context of these prohibitions, reaching out with curiosity, to better understand the rabbinic sources and methodology. In general, I believe that clergy are feeling more permission and empowerment to name how bad the track record has been and try to make amends for denying LGBTQ folks access to sacred spaces.

I think the greatest recent shift has come from the proximity of people who have LGBTQ family members, particularly young people who don't want to choose between a religious identity and a queer identity, staying within the community. Another is the awareness of how prevalent, and horrific, the rabbinic malpractice of asking queer folks to marry in straight, mixed orientation marriages has been. There needs to be better answers to these questions.

The good news is that the edge continues to move, and quickly. When I first started doing this work, a lot of the counseling was with individuals who were struggling to better understand themselves and their identity within a religious world view. Over time it extended to helping them come out to their parents and supporting the family in the process of acceptance. Now, the most frequent questions are around marriage and speaking to communities, and extended families, who want to be part of celebrating and welcoming a new young couple.

It's amazing to witness, in our own lifetimes, how quickly this change is happening. What just a few years ago was seen as an "intolerable deviance", in that if a person came out then they needed to get out, has moved to a "tolerable deviance"; being told "I'm not ok with what you are doing, but I'd rather you be here than not". That progress took thirty-five hundred years. To go from there to "acceptance" and then "celebration" happens much faster. Often weeks or months. Sometimes even less.

What does your work as a scholar-in-residence entail?

Unfortunately, there is more work than there is time in the day. As we continue to succeed in bringing awareness of allyship as spiritual practice, and the role of clergy in helping improve the lives of LGBTQ folks, the volume increases. Each conversation is different and very situation specific. We are meant to answer people, not questions.

There is also a lot of writing. I try to publish in as many different, and diverse publications, as I can. Jewish and non-Jewish spaces. When we think about systemic change, Orthodoxy is a sliver within Judaism, which is a sliver within the religious world, which is only a part of humanity. So if we want to change the world, I think it is important to be in conversation with, and have a presence in, as much of that as possible.

Speaking publicly is a big part of this as well. In academic spaces, think tanks, and conference circuits—I think having representation from a progressive religious place is powerful and adds to the depth of perspectives.

You have acknowledged that there has been a lot of recent change, but the texts and verses themselves haven't changed. So what do you think is responsible for it?

There are some things that are not at all ambiguous, within the Hebrew Bible, but our take on reality is often quite distorted. For example, when I was younger many of my rabbis smoked cigarettes. For a significant amount of time people thought that smoking was healthy, and so many people smoked. Then, we got the memo that actually it isn't healthy at all and it can actually kill you. As a result, it became forbidden to start smoking. Jewish Law didn't change, but our understanding of reality did.

One can't appropriately answer a question in Jewish Law, until the reality is properly understood. The struggle to understand what is truly essential about gender is still ongoing to this day. Where does it really lie? Do we even have access to that knowledge? There are many questions that we don't have answers to.

As our grasp on these truths evolve and mature over time, our applications of Jewish Law will as well. Although LGBTQ identities are not new, the modern movement certainly is. It's barely fifty years from Stonewall and many of the questions being asked today were not possible to ask before now. I don't believe that rabbis could have imagined the verse about wearing misgendered clothing in the context of transgender experiences.

Trans folks, by wearing gender affirming clothing, are presenting to the world their genuine and authentic selves, the exact opposite of the prohibition. It is clear, in the commentaries and rabbinic authorities, that it is the licentious and nefarious intentions that are viewed as perverse.

It is particularly those verses that have been used to hurt and exclude people, when freed from the phobic lenses, that are the most generative in providing support and guidance on these topics.

Do you think that one of the reasons that the Jewish community has had such potent homophobia, in the past, is in part due to the influence from the outside world?

Yes. Often people want to frame this conversation, of homophobia, as a uniquely Orthodox problem. But it isn't true. Just a few decades ago this existed throughout all of Judaism. If you take a look at the responsa that were written by the Reform Movement in the 1980's these questions are framed like, "Is it acceptable to permit homosexuals to pray in Reform Synagogues?" and the answers were just as offensive. Things like, "It is good to have sinners among us when we pray."

When Rabbi Kleinbaum, the Senior Rabbi at CBST, wanted to go to Rabbi school, the Conservative Movement wasn't accepting women and the Reform Movement wasn't accepting lesbians. She chose to go to a Reconstructionist seminary even though she attended an Orthodox high school.

This is true about other denominations as well as other religions that don't feel bound to any other verse in the Hebrew Bible, and seem to care deeply about Leviticus 18:22. I was once on a panel with two other clergy, all three of us observed the Sabbath on a different day of the week, but somehow this verse everyone wants to believe in! In other words, it is not the verse that generated the homophobia, but it is a convenient place to hang it, hypocrisy notwithstanding.

Are you able to speak to the different attitudes that the Ultra Orthodox community has towards the LGB identities, as opposed to the transgender identity?

I have found that it is often cultural or community specific, however there is consistently less pushback to lesbians than there is to queer men. In general, there has been an increased level of sensitivity around the trans experience, in right leaning religious spaces, and less movement for LGB issues overall. Perhaps because it is perceived as being newer and less influenced by pre-existing positions.

There is also the presence of a rigidity of gender roles, in the Ultra Orthodox world, that in some ways supports the binary experience of trans folks; providing a certain sympathy for someone placed "in the wrong body". Traditionally, rabbis have responded to young queer men by challenging their assertions "How do you even know? You have never been with a woman before!" Reassuring them that everyone has tests in life, and this is simply theirs. It is often accompanied by encouraging, albeit offensive, words: "You'll see, she will cook and clean for you...plenty of *cholent*!"

In more modern circles, although there is less investment in gender roles and increased effort working towards greater inclusion of women in rabbinic spaces, the transgender piece does seem to be more threatening, perhaps because of the consciousness around the struggle for gender equality. Questions like, "what does it mean to be a woman?" or "as a woman I'm not good enough, but if I transition then I am?" seem more relevant in those spaces.

Overall, these questions are sourced more in people's level of comfort than an attempt to understand the Divine Will. Someone once said, "Where there is a rabbinic will, there is a *halachic* (Jewish Law) way." It is the transphobia and homophobia that is the problem, not any particular verse.

The Torah testifies about Joseph's brother that "they saw him from afar and sought to do him harm". From a distance, it is easier to dehumanize. When there is someone who you already love, and they happen to be queer or gender queer, it forces a person to face and question their prejudices.

Do you think that if you didn't have someone in your family come out as trans, that you would be as open to understanding as you are now?

I don't think so. I was never transphobic. In general I don't think that I am entitled to a vote on the lives that others live, but I don't think I ever knew someone that was out as trans before. After I started speaking about it, folks would come up to me privately and tell me that they were also trans. I always felt a sense of shock. Particularly in my own complacency in a world that encouraged people to hide who they are.

As a rule, we think about the things that affect us or are relevant to our lives. As someone who is cisgender and straight, I really couldn't gain any traction in understanding. Even now, after I have obsessively thought about this for years, I think I've gotten to the evolved place of now knowing that I just don't know. Being cis, for me, has with it a limited awareness of gender—confined to my own body.

Today I was speaking to a man, who is trans, and he has a child who is gender queer. He said to me "Rabbi, I just don't understand this." I responded "This you don't understand? I don't understand any of it!" It can actually be much more helpful, in that space, because we can become open to listening and better understand how we can be supportive.

Knowing that I don't know has made it much easier to engage in a humble questioning of it all. We can each have thoughts and perspectives to share with others, but in the end there is a lot more that we just don't have answers for.

I grew up in a Modern Orthodox community that was very clearly against same sex marriages. That has begun to shift slowly. Do you ever see that changing in the Ultra Orthodox world?

I think that there will be Ultra Orthodox queer weddings in the future. I'm not sure that I can picture the rabbis showing up to officiate, but the reality is that there are queer folks in every community and many of them want to be in committed relationships with someone of the same gender. We joke that there is one in every *minyan* (quorum of 10). If someone has twelve kids, there is a statistical likelihood that at least one of them is LGBTQ.

I've done weddings of Orthodox women and people showed up. Hundreds of people, centrist Orthodox people, attended. Not everyone was completely comfortable with it all, but they were there smiling. At one wedding, as people started to arrive, I asked the father of one of the brides how he was doing. He said, "I'm trying to get there." By the time the first dance had ended he looked over to me and said, "I got there." Because love is love. When you have two consenting adults who love each other, and want the community to bear witness to that love and commitment, it is a powerful and holy thing to observe.

Often when parents come into my office to talk about a response to their daughter coming out as gay, after seminary, my first question is usually "Is she still observant?" They will generally say yes and I will follow up with, "Well you have a choice: you can either have a lesbian daughter who is *shomer shabbos*, or a lesbian daughter who isn't *shomer shabbos*, because only one of those identities is a choice."

As the broader community begins to understand the realities of folks not wanting to choose between these identities, they can develop ways of being supportive and inclusive. At the intersection of tradition and invitation there is a lot of tension. If we change the rules too much, it is a different game. However, if we don't adapt them, no one might show up to play.

An example of a communal shift, that reflects a healthy recalibration of standards and expectation, is around intermarriage. It used to be that not being able to receive an *aliyah,* to the Torah, was a deterrent for a guy not to marry his non-Jewish girlfriend. So the custom was to enforce that policy for what was perceived as the greater good.

I don't know exactly when it lost its power to influence dating criteria, but it has been a while. As a result, today, not only isn't there a prohibition to offer an *aliyah,* to a man who married a non-Jewish woman, but the outreach and engagement is even prioritized. What was used as a tool of exclusion has now been repurposed to bring the same people closer.

In cases like this, it isn't that Jewish law changed—but our attitude and posture. Better understanding the consequences of these rulings, through the accumulation of additional points of data (often negative), provide a set of checks and balances on rabbinic guidance. Unfortunately, the trail of trauma from rabbinic negligence and malpractice is long and filled with collateral casualties. The lessons that we have learned from these missteps must inform the guidance which is offered in the future.

What do you think the immediate future holds for LGBT people whose communities are not going to embrace marriage equality in the next twenty years?

So twenty years is like a lifetime in queer years. If we think about
the modern LGBTQ movement, it is really only about fifty years
old, counting from Stonewall in 1969. When CBST started, in 1973,
people asked how it was even possible to have a gay synagogue.
Now people question why it is even necessary. This dynamic shift
has happened in all of the movements, and it is now Orthodoxy's
turn.

Most immediately, I think the urgent need to stop asking queer
folks to marry straight needs to be prioritized. I had a really horrible
case recently, when I was in Israel. A young *chassid*, maybe eighteen
years old, reached out completely distraught and crying
uncontrollably. His boyfriend had just gotten engaged to a young
woman (also a teenager), through an arranged marriage.

He was obviously upset that their relationship was going to end, I
don't think he wanted to be some side guy, but he was genuinely
concerned for the young woman who didn't know that her fiancé
was gay and was caving into the pressure from his family to get
married. It is horrific. Everyone involved there loses.

In a clear mark of progress, there are many more rabbis now who
will not officiate at a straight wedding if they know that the groom
is gay. I know how shockingly low this bar is, but it is actually an
important advancement. It is really important, beyond the obvious,
because it reinforces the reality that there are queer folks within the
Orthodox world.

The more that rabbis are aware of LGBTQ Jews, and their needs,
the easier it becomes to be helpful and supportive. In the Upper
West Side of Manhattan there are many queer couples who are
completely observant, and their presence in the community informs
and is part of the rabbinic conversation.

These beautiful families, many with children, have done so much to destigmatize the issue, by just being themselves, within the community. I think that in most Orthodox communities this will be the last generation that will be able to truthfully claim that they never knew an out, orthodox couple. That might even be too generous. Most people today know someone in their immediate family that is part of a queer community.

A very famous Rosh Yeshiva, in the Five Towns of NY, told me a few years ago that he would never throw out a child from his school just because they had two mommies or two *tatties*. Once you have kids in *cheder*, whose parents are queer, then everyone in the class is already being raised with an awareness of these identities and hopefully won't have to suffer the way that previous generations did.

We are living at a moment where the opportunity exists to break this cycle of inherited trauma. I think the time for plausible deniability has expired. Rabbis that claim that queerness can be cured simply are not being taken seriously anymore. It isn't a sustainable model anymore. You can't embrace people while asking them to be someone they are not.

Can you please tell us a little more about the work you are doing to fight conversion therapy within religious spaces?

The good news is that, because it is so horrific, it doesn't require that much convincing. A big part of the work is amplifying the voices of survivors and making sure that their stories are heard. There are many films and documentaries that have captured some of these "therapies". They are traumatizing and deeply painful to watch.

If you think that homosexuality is the work of the devil, then it shouldn't be surprising that the remedy looks like an exorcism. There is no science to support the success of such an approach, and it is literally considered a form of torture by many human rights experts.

An unintended benefit that has emerged, in reframing these conversations, is in the revelation that some of the most homophobic advocates, and practitioners, are repressed homosexuals themselves. When one of the leading Orthodox therapists was outed by a former patient, for trolling the internet for gay sex, he doubled down by saying, "While I was finding so much success in healing my patience from their traumas, that caused same sex attraction, I was clearly neglecting my own." Maybe. The stories of those who have experienced these atrocities are much more compelling than the ones trying to convince us that they work.

A prominent Modern Orthodox Rabbi, who is out about having a gay son, wrote about conversion therapy a few months ago that is really at the place where many people are at this moment. He said something like "If conversion therapy really worked, in making queer folks straight, then every queer person would be obligated to get help in becoming straight. However, because it doesn't help, it is forbidden to put someone through that trauma." It is a strange balance of being able to maintain a certain degree of homophobia, while simultaneously acknowledging that being queer isn't a choice and there isn't really anything to do about it.

On a slightly different topic, the Ultra Orthodox world has gotten a fair amount of negative attention recently. The *NY Times* article about the failures in the educational system and Netflix shows. Can you speak a bit about it?

I very much identify as part of that world. It is where I was educated and it is where the people that I look up to and try to be like are found. Aspirationally, it is where I would like for my family to continue in their religious practices. I also invest a lot of time and effort in changing it so that the best parts of it can continue, just without the homo-/trans-phobic components of it. So these articles and documentaries only tell part of a story. The Ultra Orthodox world is a beautiful one that has many amazing aspects of it. The passion of spiritual commitments and fervor is deeply inspirational, for me. And there are some deficiencies in the culture. A lot of work is still needed to fix it.

When God's house was destroyed, nearly 2,000 years ago in Jerusalem, the different assets were divided up. We all come from a broken home, with a lot of inherited trauma. In the last several generations, the left has taken "*tikkun olam*"—healing the world, while the right has focused on "*limmud HaTorah*"—learning Torah and ritual practice. Now we are observing a lot of reclaiming and blending of things that historically were never found together. There is queer Talmud and queer mikvah. Many things are shifting and intersecting in ways that were never really found before.

It is always sad for me to read these articles because there is so much good, holiness, and beauty in these communities. And no community is perfect and everyone has their issues. These articles rarely highlight the exceptional level of kindness and generosity that exists there. So much individual volunteerism and organizations that help and support people in difficult situations. It is incredible. The thoughtful charity and resources for folks struggling is remarkable.

Two final questions: What advice would you share for LGBTQ Jews who are dealing with this struggle of LGBTQ

**identity and Jewish Identity? And what advice would you give
to someone who wants to be a good ally?**

For those who find themselves as part of the LGBTQ community
and are struggling, particularly transgender youth, we see you. We
love you. God doesn't put extra people in this world, we need you.
And it does get better. It does get better.

I think the role of allies here is first to listen. To better understand
what people are going through and how to best be supportive to
remove the burden. It is not enough to help shoulder it. We can't
be complacent and feel like all is well because someone is now a
little less oppressed. It is about creating a world where there is no
oppression.

Rabbi Mike Moskowitz

Kamtza and Bar Kamtza: The Destructive Consequence of Inaction

When my Rebbe, Rav Nachman Bulman Z"l (my son Nachi's namesake), passed away, the Rosh Yeshiva, Rav Nota Schiller Shlit'a, eulogized him with a teaching from Rav Aharon of Karlin.[422] The Mishnah says:

יְהוּדָה בֶן תֵּימָא אוֹמֵר, הֱוֵי עַז כַּנָּמֵר, וְקַל כַּנֶּשֶׁר, וְרָץ כַּצְּבִי, וְגִבּוֹר כָּאֲרִי, לַעֲשׂוֹת רְצוֹן אָבִיךָ שֶׁבַּשָּׁמָיִם. הוּא הָיָה אוֹמֵר, עַז פָּנִים לְגֵיהִנֹּם, וּבֹשֶׁת פָּנִים לְגַן עֵדֶן. יְהִי רָצוֹן מִלְּפָנֶיךָ ה' אֱלֹקֵינוּ שֶׁתִּבְנֶה עִירְךָ בִּמְהֵרָה בְיָמֵינוּ וְתֵן חֶלְקֵנוּ בְתוֹרָתֶךָ:

Judah ben Tema said: Be bold as a leopard, and swift as an eagle, and fleet as a gazelle, and brave as a lion, to do the will of your Father who is in heaven. He used to say: one who is bold-faced/insolent is headed for Gehinnom, the netherworld,

---

[422] Known as Reb Aharon HaGadol and the author of the Bais Aharon (1736–1772).

and the shy for the Garden of Eden. May it be the will, O Lord our God, that your city be rebuilt speedily in our days and set our portion in the studying of your Torah.

The Beis Aharon reads the text to mean that one who has the holy pride and confidence of their mission, as an emissary of the Divine, can be sent to the most hellish places in this world and they will be successful in transforming it to a sanctuary. However, someone who is shy—בֹּשֶׁת—and lacks the conviction of their contribution—such a person should retire to the safe paradise of the study hall.[423]

Standing up for what is right requires courage and the willingness to be ridiculed for defending the dignity of those dehumanized by society. In the story of Kamtza and Bar Kamtza, the Rabbis are silent and unresponsive while they witness the shaming of Kamtza, and in so doing they contribute to his humiliation.

It is recorded in Gitten as follows:

אַקַּמְצָא וּבַר קַמְצָא חָרוּב יְרוּשְׁלַיִם דְּהַהוּא גַּבְרָא דְּרָחֲמֵיהּ קַמְצָא וּבְעֵל דְּבָבֵיהּ בַּר קַמְצָא עֲבַד סְעוֹדְתָּא אָמַר לֵיהּ לְשַׁמָּעֵיהּ זִיל אַיְיתִי לִי קַמְצָא אֲזַל אַיְיתִי לֵיהּ בַּר קַמְצָא

אָתָא אַשְׁכְּחֵיהּ דַּהֲוָה יָתֵיב אָמַר לֵיהּ מִכְּדֵי הָהוּא גַּבְרָא בְּעֵל דְּבָבָא דְּהַהוּא גַּבְרָא הוּא מַאי בָּעֵית הָכָא קוּם פּוֹק אָמַר לֵיהּ הוֹאִיל וַאֲתַאי שְׁבְקֵן וְיָהֵיבְנָא לָךְ דְּמֵי מָה דְּאָכֵילְנָא וְשָׁתֵינָא

---

[423] Internally, the Mishnah needs an explanation to account for the praise of the trait in the beginning of the teaching "עַז כַּנָּמֵר".

202

אֲמַר לֵיהּ לָא אֲמַר לֵיהּ יָהֵיבְנָא לָךְ דְּמֵי פַּלְגָא דִסְעוֹדְתָּיךְ אֲמַר לֵיהּ לָא אֲמַר לֵיהּ יָהֵיבְנָא לָךְ דְּמֵי כּוּלַּהּ סְעוֹדְתָּיךְ אֲמַר לֵיהּ לָא נַקְטֵיהּ בִּידֵיהּ וְאוֹקְמֵיהּ וְאַפְּקֵיהּ

אֲמַר הוֹאִיל וַהֲווֹ יָתְבֵי רַבָּנַן וְלָא מַחוּ בֵּיהּ שְׁמַע מִינָּהּ קָא נִיחָא לְהוּ אֵיזִיל אֵיכוֹל בְּהוּ קוּרְצָא בֵּי מַלְכָּא אֲזַל אֲמַר לֵיהּ לְקֵיסָר מָרַדוּ בָּךְ יְהוּדָאֵי אֲמַר לֵיהּ מִי יֵימַר אֲמַר לֵיהּ שַׁדַּר לְהוּ קוּרְבָּנָא חֲזֵית אִי מַקְרְבִין לֵיהּ

As a result of Kamtza and Bar Kamtza, Jerusalem was destroyed. A certain man, who had a friend named Kamtza, and an enemy named Bar Kamtza, made a banquet. He instructed his assistant "Go and invite Kamtza". He [mistakenly] invited Bar Kamtza.

[The host] finds [Bar Kamtza] sitting there and says to him "Look, that man [Bar Kamtza] is the enemy of me. What do you want here?! Get out!"

[Bar Kamtza replies] "Since I'm already here, let me stay and I will give you money for whatever I eat and drink."

"No!"

"I will give you the cost of half of your banquet."

"No!"

"I will give you the cost of the entire banquet."

"No!"

[The host] grabbed hold of [Bar Kamtza] with his hand, stood him up and threw him out. [Bar Kamtza] said [to himself] since the Rabbis were seated and didn't rebuke him, it is clear that it was acceptable to them. I will go and speak of them in the royal palace. He went and told Caesar "The Jews have rebelled against you." [Caesar asks] "Who says?" [Bar Kamtza responds] "Send them a sacrifice and see if they offer it."...

The rabbis fail to advocate for human dignity, the most basic of Jewish values. The narrative concludes with a statement about misplaced embarrassment—בּוּשָׁה:

תַּנְיָא אָמַר רַבִּי אֶלְעָזָר בֹּא וּרְאֵה כַּמָּה גְּדוֹל(ה) כֹּחָהּ שֶׁל בּוּשָׁה שֶׁהֲרֵי סִיַּיע הַקָּדוֹשׁ בָּרוּךְ הוּא אֶת בַּר קַמְצָא וְהֶחֱרִיב אֶת בֵּיתוֹ וְשָׂרַף אֶת הֵיכָלוֹ

It is taught: Rabbi Elazar says: Come and see how great is the power of shame, for the Holy One, Blessed be God, assisted bar Kamtza, God destroyed God's Temple and burned God's Sanctuary.

While the traditional understanding is that God is sympathetic to those who are shamed by others, and consequently, bar Kamtza who suffers humiliation gains Divine support even for spiritual destruction, an alternative message might be that it is the rabbinic failure to overcome their own perceived sense of shame in doing the right thing that is the cause for God's reaction.

It is perhaps for this reason that this Mishnah concludes its teaching about these emotions with an aspirational prayer: May it be your will, O Lord our God, that your city be rebuilt speedily in our days and set our portion in the studying of your Torah—highlighting the cause of the destruction, and the path towards rebuilding constructed with the confidence that embodied learning provides. Shockingly, this Mishnah is the only one in all of *Shas* that contains a prayer of יְהִי רָצוֹן מִלְּפָנֶיךָ—"May it be your will".[424]

What is so powerful about this attribute that it inhibited the Rabbis from speaking up, persuaded God into acts of destruction, and offers us the promise of redemption?

The editors of the Talmud deliberately arranged the placement of this story in the Tractate of Gitten, which deals primarily with issues of divorce, to equate the destruction of the Temple, and the subsequent exiles, with the subject of separation.[425] Rabbi Yochanan[426] introduces this *sugya* by quoting a verse in Proverbs:

אָמַר רַבִּי יוֹחָנָן מַאי דִּכְתִיב אַשְׁרֵי אָדָם מְפַחֵד תָּמִיד וּמַקְשֶׁה לִבּוֹ יִפּוֹל בְּרָעָה אַקַּמְצָא וּבַר קַמְצָא חֲרוּב יְרוּשָׁלַיִם

Rabbi Yochanan said: What is the meaning of that which is written: "Happy is the man who fears always, but he who hardens his heart shall fall into mischief"?[427] Jerusalem was destroyed on account of Kamtza and bar Kamtza."

This verse, independent of the reference to the story, requires an explanation: How is a constant state of anxiety the source of happiness? Additionally, the converse of happiness is sadness; how

---

[424] Also language of Ma Ben in Mishnah before. See Derech Chaim 482
[425] Reb Tzadok.
[426] Gittin 55b.
[427] Proverbs 28:14.

does "mischief"—בְּרָעָה—literally evil or harm—correlate to absence of fear or a soft heart?

In our pursuit of truth, if we are at all successful, we will encounter new information that will challenge aspects of our behavior and potentially threaten the continuation of certain practices. If we are humble and curious about what we do not yet know, we should be open and excited to learn more and not be deterred by the consequences of the newly acquired knowledge. The only fear is missing out on the opportunity to mature and evolve into a more perfect person.

The first letter of each word, in Hebrew, for the person who is always afraid, spells the word "truth" אמת—אָדָם מְפַחֵד תָּמִיד.[428] If our hearts are open to learn more, we are happy to be aware of and connected to a more informed reality. When Pharaoh is confronted by the existence of God, and the miraculous events of the plagues, he "hardens his heart" as a way of continuing on his path as if the world around him is actually his fictitious world of make believe. Of course, such a hardening of the heart doesn't end well for him, or the Egyptians that he forces to follow him.

Being in a loving relationship requires an attentiveness to the other, and a healthy amount of concern for the wellbeing of all involved. If we see the Torah as a "tree of life to those who support it" we shouldn't want any space between what the Torah teaches is good and the way we live our lives. We should strive to be *talmidei chachamim*, practitioners of the wisdom.

---

[428] See Chasam Sofer.

This is why the blessings over the study of Torah, that one recites in the morning, apply to all of the Torah learned throughout the day. Even if a person is engaged in work or other activities throughout the day there should be a constant process of thinking about the right thing to do in each moment, so that when the time comes to properly study Torah later in the day, the continuity of consciousness of the original blessing remains.

The Talmud,[429] in tractate Nedarim, attributes the loss of the Temple to the failure to recite the blessings before learning— שֶׁאֵין מְבָרְכִין בַּתּוֹרָה תְּחִלָּה. One understanding of this teaching is that the study of Torah became separate from the way that folks were living their lives. They would go about their business and when they would return to learn in the evenings, it was like a new experience which would require a new blessing.[430]

An additional introduction to the story comes from the beginning of Nedarim:[431]

מִקְדָּשׁ רִאשׁוֹן מִפְּנֵי מָה חָרַב—מִפְּנֵי שְׁלֹשָׁה דְּבָרִים שֶׁהָיוּ בּוֹ: עֲבוֹדָה זָרָה, וְגִלּוּי עֲרָיוֹת, וּשְׁפִיכוּת דָּמִים. ...אֲבָל מִקְדָּשׁ שֵׁנִי שֶׁהָיוּ עוֹסְקִין בְּתוֹרָה וּבְמִצְוֹת וּגְמִילוּת חֲסָדִים, מִפְּנֵי מָה חָרַב? מִפְּנֵי שֶׁהָיְתָה בּוֹ שִׂנְאַת חִנָּם. לְלַמֶּדְךָ שֶׁשְּׁקוּלָה שִׂנְאַת חִנָּם כְּנֶגֶד שָׁלֹשׁ עֲבֵירוֹת: עֲבוֹדָה זָרָה, גִּלּוּי עֲרָיוֹת, וּשְׁפִיכוּת דָּמִים

Due to what reason was the First Temple destroyed? It was destroyed due to the fact that there were three matters that existed in the First Temple: Idol worship, forbidden sexual

---

[429] Nedarim 81a.
[430] See Ran.
[431] 9b also see Jerusalem Talmud.

relations, and bloodshed…However, during the Second Temple they were engaged in Torah, mitzvot, and acts of kindness, [and not the sins of the First Temple] why was it destroyed? Due to baseless hatred. This teaches you that baseless hatred is equivalent to the three transgressions: Idol worship, forbidden sexual relations and bloodshed.

This baseless hatred manifested in the form of *lashon hara*—or speaking badly about people,[432] and even about the Land of Israel.[433] Speaking negatively isn't a positive trait, but it is the underlying worldview that is most problematic. Rav Chaim Shmuelevitz[434] notes that Israel is condemned to wander the desert for forty years, corresponding to the forty days of the scouting mission. This is because they carried their negative worldview with them right from the start.[435]

Our actions in any particular moment, while not the totality of who we are, reflect our identity more broadly. The incident of Kamtza and bar Kamtza is emblematic of the dominant culture of the time. While the technical moment brought about the destruction of the Temple in that generation, it reflects a systemic issue of the Jewish people at that time and continuing to this day.

Kamtza and bar Kamtza, who according to some are possibly father and son,[436] represent a breakdown in the collective and a blatant disregard for others. This is alluded to in the name

---

[432] See introduction to the Sefer Chafitz Chaim.
[433] Tanis 29a teaches that the spies gave their negative report on the 9th of Av and contributed to the future destruction of the Temple.
[434] Rosh Yeshivah of the Mir (1902–1979).
[435] See Sichos Mussar page 158.
[436] See Maharsha.

"Kamtza" meaning to clench or selfishly grab.[437] Although Kamtza is not actually part of the explicit interaction detailed in the Talmud,[438] he is held equally accountable. The Ben Yehoyada explains: דכל מי שיש בידו למחות ולא מיחה נקרא הדבר על שמו—"anyone who has the capacity to protest, and doesn't, is given attribution [for the negative act] by name."[439]

The anonymous host is not the center or subject of the story; we don't even know his name. He is simply a placeholder for the evil of the moment that we are called to answer. As passive observers, the rabbis' hearts were hardened by their wealth and privilege.[440] This temporary comfort obfuscated their thinking about the future consequences of their inaction.[441]

Individuals must be willing to defy the majority, if the majority is corrupt.[442] "לֹא־תִהְיֶה אַחֲרֵי־רַבִּים לְרָעֹת וְלֹא־תַעֲנֶה עַל־רִב לִנְטֹת אַחֲרֵי רַבִּים לְהַטֹּת׃"—You should not go after the many to do bad; and you shall not respond over a dispute to favor after the many." It also connects the story of the spies to the dinner party, by highlighting the need for courageous faith.

When Moses changes Hoshea's name to "Joshua", in preparation for scouting out the land,[443] it is motivated by the fear that Joshua is

---

[437] There are many opinions about the etymology of this word. See Minchas Asher and Maharsha.

[438] There is a dispute if he was actually at the party or not. Ben Ish Chai holds that he was there.

[439] It is noteworthy that the host in the narrative remains anonymous.

[440] See Tosafot—"Happy is the person who is afraid".

[441] See Rashi—"Happy is the person who is afraid".

[442] Exodus 23:2.

[443] Numbers 13:16.

too humble.[444] Rashi explains that Moses prayed on behalf of Joshua that he shouldn't succumb to the peer pressure of the spies. This continues to the very end of Moses' life when he summoned Joshua, in front of all of Israel, and tells him "Be strong and have courage—חֲזַק וֶאֱמָץ".[445]

Discerning when it is appropriate to tolerate, accept, and even celebrate people that we strongly disagree with, and when that posture of inclusivity betrays our beliefs is a complex exercise. Being intolerant of hate and evil is an essential component of our spiritual practice—"Those who love God hate evil!—אֹהֲבֵי ה' שִׂנְאוּ־רָע",[446] and isn't actually in tension with our value of unity, but knowing where to draw those lines is not always clear.

Moses is famously described as "exceedingly humble, more so than any other human being on earth—וְהָאִישׁ מֹשֶׁה עָנָו מְאֹד מִכֹּל הָאָדָם אֲשֶׁר עַל־פְּנֵי הָאֲדָמָה."[447] Rashi explains that Moses's *anuva* was "humble and patient—שָׁפָל וְסַבְלָן". However, when the Talmud quotes Rabbi Yochanan's claim that it was Rabbi Zekharya ben Avkolas's humility—*anuva*—that destroyed the Temple: " אָמַר רַבִּי יוֹחָנָן שֶׁל רַבִּי זְכַרְיָה בֶּן אַבְקוּלָס הֶחֱרִיבָה אֶת בֵּיתֵנוּ וְשָׂרְפָה אֶת הֵיכָלֵנוּ עִנְוְותָנוּתוֹ סבלנותו שסבל את זה—Rashi frames it as a deficiency: וְהִגְלִיתָנוּ מֵאַרְצֵנוּ ולא הרגו—His patience, since he tolerated this one…".[448]

Moses wasn't humble because he felt inadequate or under-resourced. It was his unique proximity and understanding of the

---

444 Targum Yonason ben Uziel.
445 Deuteronomy 31:7.
446 Psalms 97:10.
447 Numbers 12:3.
448 Gittin 56a.

unparalleled greatness of the Divine that offered him the
perspective of his proper place. Moses was aware of the power of
God and God's goodness that assisted him in both confidently
aligning with good against evil, and having the patient tolerance for
those journeying in a different direction.

Loving another and making space for them is not a compromise of
our personal truth or convictions. Destruction, however, comes
through the hate that we have for those who are different.
Lamentations begins "אֵיכָה יָשְׁבָה בָדָד הָעִיר"—Alas! Lonely sits the
city". The first letter of each word forms איבה—"animosity".[449]

King Solomon[450] offers some advice to encourage transitioning
from hate to love:

"בִּרְצוֹת ה' דַּרְכֵי־אִישׁ גַּם־אוֹיְבָיו יַשְׁלִם אִתּוֹ"—When Hashem favors a
person's ways, even their enemies will make peace with them." This
is understood by the Rabbis to mean that when a person wants to
be aligned with God, the way to achieve that is by making peace
with one's enemies—"אם חפץ שירצה דרכו הקדוש ברוך הוא, ישלם הוא
בעצמו על אויביו".

Failing to find a compromise, between two people in dispute, is also
blamed for the Temple being destroyed.[451] " דאמר ר' יוחנן לא חרבה
ירושלים אלא על שדנו בה דין תורה אלא דיני דמגיזתא לדיינו אלא אימא
שהעמידו דיניהם על דין תורה ולא עבדו לפנים משורת הדין—as Rabbi
Yochanan says: Jerusalem was destroyed only for the fact that they

---

[449] See Reishis Chochma Gate of Humility 4.
[450] Proverbs 16:7.
[451] See Meor Einie Chachamim on Perkie Avos.

adjudicated cases on the basis of Torah law in the city, and not beyond the letter of the law (*peshara*—compromise).[452]

The *midrash* reinforces this trajectory with an incremental arc to achieve love of humanity.[453] It posits that the beginning of fear is shame, followed by humility, and ultimately a love for God's creations.[454] If we understand the shame to be an embarrassment for the current state of the world, then the path towards happiness is marked by the constant state of concern for how the world is treating people.

Our strength comes from our connection to the Creator, and the power of that relationship is determined by how much we believe in its reality. May it be your will, O Lord our God, that your city be rebuilt speedily in our days and set our portion in the studying of your Torah.

---

[452] Bava Metzia 30b.
[453] Tanna D'Bei Eliyahu Zuta introduction.
[454] The seven steps are:

תחלת יראה בושה, שנייה לה ענוה, שלישית לה אומנות נקייה, רביעית לה רחמנות, חמישית לה קיום מצות, שישית לה רדיפת שלום, שביעית לה אהבת הבריות.

Made in United States
North Haven, CT
19 March 2023